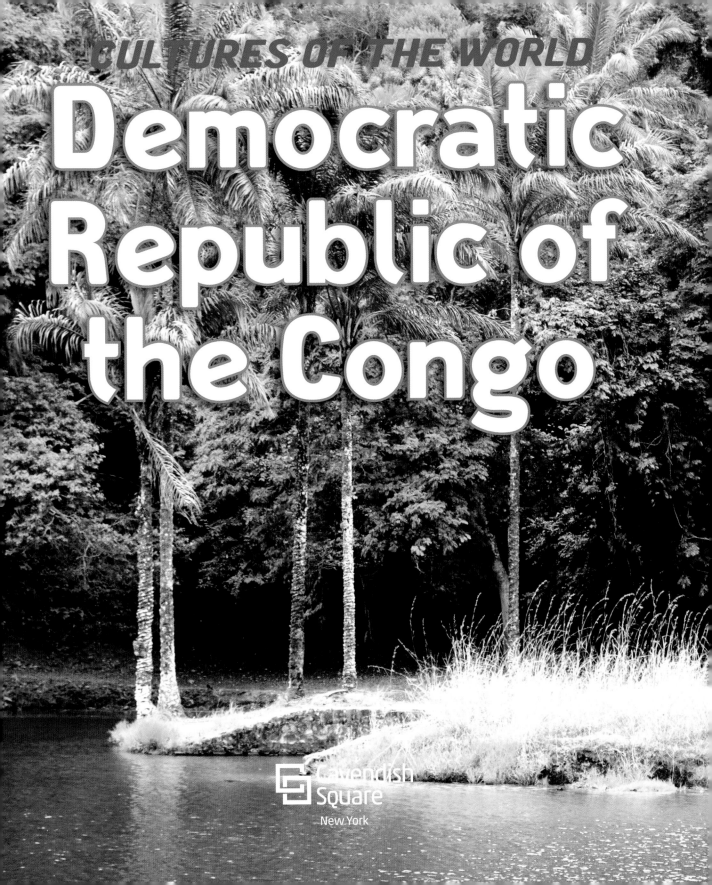

CULTURES OF THE WORLD

Democratic Republic of the Congo

Cavendish Square

New York

Published in 2019 by Cavendish Square Publishing, LLC
243 5th Avenue, Suite 136, New York, NY 10016
Copyright © 2019 by Cavendish Square Publishing, LLC

Third Edition

Cataloging-in-Publication Data

Names: Heale, Jay. | Jui Lin, Yong. | Nevins, Debbie.
Title: Democratic Republic of the Congo / Jay Heale, Yong Jui Lin, and Debbie Nevins.
Description: New York : Cavendish Square, 2019. | Series: Cultures of the world | Includes glossary and index.
Identifiers: LCCN ISBN 9781502636386 (library bound) | ISBN 9781502636393 (ebook)
Subjects: LCSH: Congo (Democratic Republic)--Juvenile literature.
Classification: LCC DT644 H43 2019 | DDC 967.51--dc23

Writers, Jay Heale and Yong Jui Lin; Debbie Nevins, third edition
Editorial Director, third edition: David McNamara
Editor, third edition: Debbie Nevins
Art Director, third edition: Amy Greenan
Designer, third edition: Jessica Nevins
Picture Researcher, third edition: Jessica Nevins
Printed in the United States of America

PRECEDING PAGE

A lake in the tropical rainforest of the Democratic Republic of the Congo.

Printed in the United States of America

CONTENTS

DEMOCRATIC REPUBLIC OF THE CONGO TODAY   **5**

1. GEOGRAPHY
The shape of the land • Climate • Rainfall • Congo River • Kinshasa • Mining district • Northern forests • Eastern border • Plants and animals   **9**

2. HISTORY
The Kongo kingdom • First European explorers • Belgian colonialism • Independence • The Congo Crisis • Mobutu's rule • The First Congo War • Enter Kabila • The Second Congo War • The second Kabila • Never-ending war   **23**

3. GOVERNMENT
The colonial inheritance • Congolese politics • Political struggles • The constitution • Parliamentary government • The judiciary • The armed forces   **39**

4. ECONOMY
Agriculture and food • Mining and industry • Transportation • Hydroelectric power   **49**

5. ENVIRONMENT
The ecosystem • Endangered animals • National parks • Logging • Ongoing damage to the environment   **57**

6. CONGOLESE
The ethnic groups • Characteristics • Refugees • Dress   **69**

7. LIFESTYLE
Poverty and starvation • Getting around • City life • Country life • Education • Health • The role of women   **77**

8. RELIGION   Christianity • Syncretic Christian-African religions • African traditional religions • Church and state   **87**

9. LANGUAGE   The main languages •Africanization• Greetings   **95**

10. ARTS   Music and dance • Traditional arts • Painting • Carving   **101**

11. LEISURE   Children at play • Sports • Storytelling • Nightlife   **111**

12. FESTIVALS   Patriotic holidays • Religious days • Family festivals   **117**

13. FOOD   Hunger • Malnourished children • Food supply challenges • Everyday fare • Eating out   **121**

MAP OF THE DEMOCRATIC REPUBLIC OF THE CONGO   **132**

ABOUT THE ECONOMY   **135**

ABOUT THE CULTURE   **137**

TIMELINE   **138**

GLOSSARY   **140**

FOR FURTHER INFORMATION   **141**

BIBLIOGRAPHY   **142**

INDEX   **143**

DRC TODAY

THIS IS A BEAUTIFUL COUNTRY. IT HOLDS THE GREATEST RIVER, the largest rain forests, the biggest city, and the richest mineral reserves of Central Africa. It has a multitude of extraordinary wildlife—gorillas, elephants, leopards, and hippos—and many other animals found nowhere else on earth. Wide, winding rivers; raging rapids; rainbow waterfalls; enormous lakes; and a vast network of inland waterways are the watery lifeblood of the Congo. There are even snow-topped mountains—in Africa, yes!—and active volcanoes. The Congolese people make vibrant, lively music that can get anyone's feet dancing.

By rights, the Democratic Republic of the Congo (DRC) should be a wealthy country and a tourist's paradise. And yet, the truth is a very different story.

Named after the ancient kingdom of Kongo, the beauty of this country has been marred by a history of colonial brutality, oppression, and economic exploitation. After casting off its European subjugators, the Congolese state fell victim to homegrown dictators and kleptocrats—high-powered thieves who sucked the riches right out of the very land. Half a century after finally achieving independence, the nation still suffers from bloody armed struggles, rebellion, and unrest. The Second Congo War

(1998—2003), sometimes called the African World War, caused millions of casualties, making it the deadliest conflict on earth since World War II.

This country has some of the worst roads in the world—that is, where there are roads at all. More than 2 million of its children are malnourished, its people are starving, disease is rampant, and the government is corrupt and ineffective. The fragility of the state has allowed continued conflict and human rights abuses. Interethnic conflicts have kept the eastern provinces in a nearly constant state of war, forcing hundreds of thousands of people to flee their homes in search of safety. Recent efforts at peace have been tenacious at best, and despite the intervention of United Nations peacekeepers—who themselves have been a source of trouble—the threat of a complete governmental collapse and renewed war still looms large.

The people of Congo lead a simple life and are generous at heart. But they have been robbed by their rulers and outside interests of almost every possibility of economic development. In short, the DRC—the most resource-rich country in the world by some measures—is one of the poorest countries on earth.

Is the DRC deteriorating into a so-called failed state, or is it already there? A failed state is one in which the government can no longer perform basic functions or provide public services such as education, security, or governance, usually because of ongoing violence and/or extreme poverty. A failed state cannot adequately protect its citizens from lawlessness, hunger, or foreign incursions. A failed state is often characterized by corruption at the highest levels. Tyrants and their associates personally profit mightily from the breakdown of a nation's governing infrastructures. Foreign governments can also knowingly destabilize a state by fueling ethnic warfare or supporting rebel forces, causing it to collapse. All of this is occurring in the DRC.

Is there hope for this beautiful country? Countless nations and international organizations are trying to help. In many ways, the humanitarian groups are trying to fill the vacuum left by the ineffective government—a role that is beyond their capacity.

In October 2017, the United Nations categorized the situation in the DRC a Level 3 emergency—the UN's highest level. This designation allows the

UN to focus its maximum resources on the country's colossal and complex humanitarian needs. The UN Office for the Coordination of Humanitarian Affairs (OCHA) then launched its largest ever funding appeal, but there's no assurance it will raise the necessary funds.

Humanitarian efforts, critical as they are, cannot solve the country's problems. And though one person alone cannot do so either, the Congo is in great need of a new kind of leader. Most observers agree that President Joseph Kabila has not been that person. Nevertheless, he refused to step down at the end of his term in 2016, adding yet another layer of political crisis to the Congo's burden.

Meanwhile, it is individuals like the Congolese gynecological surgeon Denis Mukwege who provide the greatest sources of hope. Mukwege, founder and director of the Panzi Hospital in Bukavu, has devoted himself to treating women who have been sexually abused and horribly traumatized. Violence against women has been—and is still being—used as a strategy of war in ethnic conflicts that are devastating the Congo, and Mukwege led the world-wide fight against such terror. For his efforts, he and his family were nearly killed in a violent assassination attempt in 2012. The good doctor, who refuses to be intimidated, has been honored with numerous international humanitarian awards and is considered a strong contender for the Nobel Peace Prize.

People like Denis Mukwege are among the Democratic Republic of the Congo's greatest resources—and therein lies the country's best chance for a better future.

DRC surgeon and humanitarian Dennis Mukwege is honored at an awards gala in New York City.

GEOGRAPHY

Animals graze in the grassy plains of the DRC.

A T THE CENTER OF THE CONTINENT of Africa is a vast country. Crisscrossed by rivers—and dominated by the mighty Congo River—it is dense with tropical rainforests, a broad plateau with mountains in the east, plains and savanna in the south, and grasslands in the north. It has one tiny arm that reaches westward to the Atlantic Ocean, but it is otherwise landlocked.

This is the Democratic Republic of the Congo (DRC), the second-largest country in Africa after Algeria. From 1971 to 1997, it was called Zaire. It's about one quarter the size of the United States and seventy-seven times as large as Belgium, the country that first colonized the area. It borders nine other countries: from the north, clockwise, the Central African Republic (CAR), South Sudan, Uganda, Rwanda, Burundi, Tanzania, Zambia, Angola, and the Republic of the Congo.

That last country, which borders the DRC to the northwest, is also named Congo, which can lead to confusion. To help alleviate the problem, the two nations are sometimes referred to as Congo- followed by their capital city. Therefore, the DRC is called Congo-Kinshasa, while the Republic of the Congo is called Congo-Brazzaville. It lies across the Congo River from the DRC and is a considerably smaller nation.

This map shows the DRC in Central Africa and it's neighbors. Notice the narrow extension reaching for the western coast, where the Congo River empties into the Atlantic Ocean.

THE SHAPE OF THE LAND

The eastern border of the DRC is clearly defined by the lakes of the Rift Valley, an ancient geological fault in eastern Africa. In the west a thin strip of land gives the country a short seacoast, only 25 miles (40 kilometers) long, where the Congo River reaches the Atlantic Ocean. Kinshasa, the capital, is some 320 miles (515 km) inland, on the southern bank of the Congo. Brazzaville, capital of the Republic of the Congo, is opposite, on the northern bank.

The center of this huge country consists of two major river basins of the Congo River (also called the Zaire River) and its many tributaries. In between and around are high plateaus, 2,000—5,000 feet (610—1,524 meters) above sea level, thick forests, and rolling, sunbaked plains. Mountain ranges stand guard in the east, and a thin wedge of coastal plain lies in the west.

CLIMATE

In such an enormous country, there are variations in climate. The central forest basin has an equatorial climate—the equator runs south of Kisangani, its location marked by a stone pillar beside the road. In this area the temperature is rarely below 80 degrees Fahrenheit (27° Celsius), with swelteringly high humidity and rain throughout the year. Rainfall totals 60—80 inches (152—203 centimeters) annually and occurs throughout the year. In the highlands to the east, it is cooler, with an average temperature of 65°F (18°C), because of the altitude. The Atlantic coast is affected by the cold Benguela current, which reduces the heat and humidity from time to time. Inland from the coast in Kinshasa, the high humidity can make visitors feel dizzy and sick. There is an almost permanent heat haze over the city, so that the sun glares from a hazy, white-hot sky. Yet in the high-plateau country in the east and the south, the prevailing winds that blow from the southeast much of the year produce lower temperatures, sometimes near freezing at night. Snow does fall in the country in the high Rwenzori Range.

RAINFALL

The average annual rainfall is around 60 inches (152 cm) in the north and about 50 inches (127 cm) in the south. The regions north of the equator have a more defined dry season from December to March and a rainy season from April to November. Areas south of the equator are dry from June to September and wet from October to May. Global warming is likely to make the climate more humid in the future, with a high risk of flooding at the estuary of the Congo River.

In January 2017, flash floods caused by the swollen Kalamu River left at least ten thousand people homeless and dozens dead or missing in Boma, a port town on the Congo River. But that was not unusual. Each year, flooding kills dozens of people in the DRC.

THE CONGO RIVER

The word *zaïre* is a traditional African name for big rivers, so this great African river is called either the Zaire or the Congo. The Congo is the second-longest river in Africa, after the Nile. It rises in the mountains near the western Rift Valley system and curves north, west, and then southwest past Kinshasa and Brazzaville to reach the Atlantic Ocean at Moanda. It crosses the equator twice, flowing through both Northern and Southern Hemisphere climatic zones; thus there is always a rainy season somewhere in its huge basin.

The potential for hydroelectric power is enormous; its water volume is second only to that of the Amazon. The main river channel is about 2,718 miles (4,374 km) long and up to 10 miles (16 km) wide. Because of its speed, rapids, and turbulence, the Congo River has never been accurately measured along much of its length. Nevertheless it is thought to be the deepest river in the world—estimates of its greatest depth vary between 722 and 820 feet (220 and 250 m).

There are more than four thousand islands in the river, many inhabited by fishermen. The main tributaries are the Ubangi in the north, which forms the border with the Republic of the Congo, and the Kasai in the south, which rises in Angola and flows northward to join the Congo upstream from Kinshasa. The Congo drains the vast Congo River Basin, an area of more than 1.6 million square miles (4.1 million square km) and, at high-water periods, discharges approximately 1.2 million cubic feet (33,980 cubic m) of water per second into the sea.

The Congo Delta is an area of lush green islands and endless reed marshes. The river is navigable for 90 miles (145 km), from its estuary to the port of Matadi. The next stretch of 186 miles (299 km) is full of rapids and waterfalls. Then the waterway is clear again from Kinshasa to Kisangani, which covers a distance of more than 1,087 miles (1,749 km).

The Congo River has many linked tributaries. It has a total of some 9,000 miles (14,484 km) of navigable inland waterways. They are used by numerous craft, from riverboats and cargo steamers to luxury yachts and dugout canoes.

KINSHASA

The capital city is situated on the Congo River at the point where river traffic heading to the coast must stop because of the rapids downstream. Passengers disembark, and cargo is off-loaded; all continue by rail toward the Atlantic Coast and the port of Matadi. Kinshasa (once called Léopoldville) is Africa's third-largest urban area after Cairo, in Egypt, and Lagos, Nigeria. It's a huge city of 11 million people, most of whom are desperately poor and constantly in search of employment.

A few rich government officials and foreign traders live in heavily guarded mansions or in hotels such as the Intercontinental. As with all other colonial towns, separate sections for Europeans and Africans were originally built, and there is still a clear distinction between the two areas. The affluent suburb of Gombe near the river has paved streets and electricity; elsewhere there are endless areas of small, square houses built of concrete blocks, roofed with rusting corrugated iron, and backed with lean-to shanties and dusty yards.

Kinshasa is regularly regarded as one of Africa's most crime-ridden cities. Crime statistics are so inconsistent as to be meaningless, with one source reporting with a homicide rate possibly as high as 112 homicides per 100,000 people, and another giving an official figure of 14 homicides per 100,000. However, all sources seem to agree that the city is quite dangerous. In its 2017 Crime and Safety Report for the DRC, the US State Department Overseas Security Advisory Council (OSAC) reported, "The US Department of State has assessed Kinshasa as being a critical threat location for crime directed at or affecting official US government interests." It went on to report, "The vast majority of criminal incidents against Americans in Kinshasa are crimes of opportunity. Nearly all are for financial gain. The most commonly reported crimes are pickpocketing, theft (from persons, vehicles, and residences), and robbery."

Pedestrians cross a wide boulevard in downtown Kinshasa.

MINING DISTRICT

The mineral-rich region of Katanga was known as Shaba from 1971 to 1997. Its industrial center is at Lubumbashi, and the entire area is rich with deposits of copper, cobalt, uranium, cadmium, tin, and zinc, as well as gold and silver. Katanga does not fully exploit this underground wealth, because of the expense involved in setting up mines and processing plants and the difficulty in transporting the processed minerals for export. Lubumbashi lies at the center of railway lines to Llebo, Kindu, Sakania, and Kolwezi; however, the railway lines are not very reliable. Many of the mining plants have been looted and all but destroyed.

Lubumbashi was built by the copper-hungry Belgians and originally named Elisabethville after their queen. It is a pretty town with wide streets and old-fashioned buildings. During the copper-boom days, Lubumbashi was one of Zaire's centers of wealth; it is still the country's second-largest city.

Mbuji-Mayi, which is a diamond-mining center, is located about halfway between Kinshasa and Lubumbashi on the Mbuji-Mayi River. One of the

A Welsh boy, John Rowlands, sailed as a cabin boy to New Orleans, where he was adopted by a cotton broker, Henry Morton Stanley, and took his name. He served in the Confederate Army in the American Civil War. Later, as a special correspondent for the New York Herald, *he accompanied a British military expedition to Ethiopia.*

The Herald sent Stanley to find David Livingstone, a British explorer who had set off to discover the source of the Nile and disappeared. Crossing Africa from Zanzibar, Stanley led an expedition of two thousand men into what Europeans then called "Darkest Africa" or the "Dark Continent"—because it was mysterious, largely unmapped, and unknown to Westerners. (Naturally, the Africans knew their own land quite well. Today the phrase is considered antiquated, Eurocentric, and even offensive.) Stanley found Livingstone on the shore of Lake Tanganyika in Tanzania on November 10, 1871, with the now-famous words, "Dr. Livingstone, I presume?"

Later, after Livingstone died, Stanley took up the cause of finding the source of the Nile. In later expeditions, Stanley sailed around Lake Victoria and Lake Tanganyika before navigating much of the Lualaba and Congo rivers. In the employ of King Léopold II of Belgium, he supervised the building of a road that runs now from Kinshasa to Kisangani. In later life, he became a British subject once again, served as a member of Parliament (1895–1900), and was knighted (1899).

Today Stanley is regarded as a controversial figure because of his service to King Léopold II, possible dealings with slave traders, and his alleged attitudes and behaviors toward African people.

country's largest urban areas has grown around the town. Here diamonds are mined legally, mostly for industrial use, as well as illegally by families who dig and sift the red soil in any unguarded valley. To reduce diamond smuggling, those not employed by the mines are required to have an official permit, but this system frequently encourages corruption.

Slag heaps, burnt earth, power pylons, and shacks made of old tin or sunbaked, earthen bricks are common features in the mining areas. The number of trees declines each month, as women harvest them for firewood. In summer the inhabitants are pestered by swarms of moisture bees, which are attracted by perspiration, and mosquitoes. Malaria is a common disease.

Tropical grasslands are brightened up with red-earth anthills, tawny grass, the occasional lush green palm tree, and pink bougainvilleas. The dense rain forest is a mixture of papaya and mango trees and cleared areas for habitation with parched, overused soil that offers little but subsistence living.

NORTHERN FORESTS

Much of the east and northeast of the country is covered with equatorial forest so thick and inhospitable to humans that it is virtually impenetrable. Although the country's untapped mineral riches are fairly well recognized, there are also riches contained in these enormous forests.

The timber includes mahogany, ebony, limba, and sapele, as well as raffia and sisal, which grow in the cleared areas. There are countless plants used by traditional healers that are gradually being recognized by modern medicine. There are rubber and palm trees, edible mushrooms that grow wild, fruit trees such as avocado and banana, and roots.

A few large-scale logging operations—mostly foreign owned—harvest the forests. The cleared areas attract settlers, but the land clearing also causes erosion, and the homes of many poverty-stricken families are at risk as numerous gullies eat their way up the hillside slopes.

The Ituri Forest in the northeast province of Ituri takes its name from the Ituri River. Largely untouched by modern development, this rainforest was made known to the outside world by the explorer Henry Morton Stanley who trekked through the region in 1887—1888.

In the northwest near the border with the Central African Republic, there was once a little-known village in the middle of the jungle. But because it was the birthplace of former president Mobutu Sese Seko, Gbadolite was built up far beyond its needs or importance. When Mobutu was at the height of his power, this "Versailles in the jungle" had the best water, electricity supply, hospital, and shopping facilities in the country. They say Mobutu flew an airplane across the Atlantic thirty-two times (at the country's expense) to Venezuela in order to pick up five thousand long-haired sheep for his Gbadolite "ranch."

After Laurent Kabila successfully led a rebellion and ousted Mobutu from power in 1997, he raided Gbadolite and looted most of the wealth in its palaces. In 1998 the Ugandan-backed Movement for the Liberation of Congo (MLC) rebel group, led by Jean-Pierre Bemba, captured Gbadolite from Kabila's government, and it became the MLC's headquarters.

Today the dilapidated palaces are overrun by vegetation, like modern ruins.

The rainforest covers about 24,300 thousand square miles (63,000 sq km), and includes the Okapi Wildlife Reserve, one of Congo's five World Heritage Sites. It is also the home of the elusive Mbuti pygmy people, who live the hunter-gatherer lifestyle of their ancient ancestors. They are characterized by their short stature, which helps them move easily through the tangled jungle growth.

KISANGANI is the largest city in the tropical forest region of the Congo, with a population of 1.602 million in 2015. Formerly known as Stanleyville, after the explorer Henry Morton Stanley, it's an important inland port on the Congo River. Being located at the farthest navigable point upriver, it's a terminus at the end of a network of river-trading stations from as far downriver as Kinshasa. The city is also a major hub for land transportation, with railroads, buses, and taxis—and Bangoka International Airport, one of the country's main airports. This ethnically-diverse urban center in the middle of the bush functions as a marketing and distribution center for the northeastern part of the country.

Kisangani was the site of the first open fighting between Ugandan and Rwandan forces during the Second Congo War (August 1998—July 2003). The fighting was in part over the gold mines near the town. As a result, Kisangani was been looted by the army on several occasions and remains very rundown and damaged. There are said to be more bicycles than cars on the battered streets, where weeds grow in potholes. Red dust covers the town in the hot season and turns to red mud during the rains.

Upriver from the city are seven major rapids; the nearest to town is Boyoma Falls, which was once called Stanley Falls. Fishermen catch perch in tall, cone-shape traps in Boyoma Falls. This region is mostly busy with farming and the raising of livestock.

EASTERN BORDER

The split in the African continent known as the Great Rift Valley forms the eastern border of the DRC. In this area there is a chain of great lakes. The once picturesque towns of Bukavu and Goma are on the shores of Lake Kivu. They are popular with visitors on their way to see the lowland gorillas in the Kahuzi-Biéga National Park or mountain gorillas in the Virunga National Park.

With such tourism potential, Goma, the capital of North Kivu province on the northern shore of Lake Kivu, was at one time "Zaire's window to the world." The airport was well equipped and presentable. After the area was overrun by Rwandan refugees in 1994 and became the starting point of resistance by Kabila's rebel army, tourism became a thing of the past. The refugees left their mark on the forest-covered hills, which in places have turned into bare, muddy ground. Every day thousands walk a little farther into the forest to chop firewood. The southern part of this border is formed by Lake Tanganyika, which is an incredibly deep freshwater lake well stocked with fish. Because of overfishing, former industrial fisheries around Lake Tanganyika have collapsed. The roads thread their way through plantations of coffee, tea, and banana palms.

On 20 November 2012, M23 rebels—also known as the Congolese Revolutionary Army—took control of Goma, with its population of one million people. The conflict, backed by Rwanda, forced more than 140,000 people to flee their homes.

MOUNTAINS

Running along the Congo's eastern border with Uganda, Rwanda, Burundi and Tanzania are the mountains of the Albertine Rift. The snow-capped Rwenzori Mountains alongside Lake Albert are spectacular and popular with climbers. The range is about 75 miles (121 km) long and 40 miles (64 km) wide. The Rwenzori are known for their vegetation (ranging from tropical rain forest to alpine meadows) and for their animal population, including forest elephants, several primate species, and many native birds. The range supports its own species and varieties of giant groundsel and giant lobelia.

The central peak, Mount Stanley, has two summits: Margherita Peak at 16,798 feet (5,120 m) and Alexandra Peak at 16,750 feet (5,105 m). It is the highest mountain in both the DRC and neighboring Uganda, and spans the border between the two countries. On the Uganda side, it is part of the Rwenzori Mountains National Park and a UNESCO World Heritage Site. On the Congo side, it is part of Virunga National Park, also a World Heritage Site. Named for the explorer Henry Morton Stanley, Mount Stanley is the third-highest mountain in Africa.

Farther south is the Mitumba Range, running north to south on the western sides of Lake Kivu and Lake Tanganyika. In this range, the two main peaks, Mount Kahuzi, with a height of 10,850 feet (3,308 m), and Mount Biéga, at 9,154 feet (2,790 m), are extinct volcanoes. Together, they are part of the Kahuzi-Biéga National Park.

PLANTS AND ANIMALS

With so much of the country inaccessible because of the tangled forests and the muddy dirt tracks that serve as roads, it is not surprising that there is a rich and varied store of vegetation and wildlife. The equatorial forests contain rubber trees, valuable hardwood timbers, and fruit trees, including bananas, coconut palms, and plantains. Tropical flowers abound; perhaps

BONOBOS

The bonobo (Pan paniscus), sometimes called the pygmy chimpanzee, is an African ape that lives exclusively in the Democratic Republic of the Congo, in the rain forests south of the Congo River. It is the closest living relative of humans. Both chimpanzees and bonobos share 98.7 percent of the same DNA as humans. The bonobo is known to be more intelligent than the other apes and is more similar to human beings in appearance.

While the larger chimpanzees roam a distinct territory in groups of about forty, the bonobos form smaller and more permanent family groups that forage on their own. Because their food (mostly fruit) is in good supply, there is little competition among the groups, and the bonobos have a more cohesive society with considerably less aggression displayed. They use simple tools such as stones and wood as hammers to break open nuts, and occasionally they hunt and eat meat.

The number of bonobos left in the wild is uncertain, but conservationists believe they are in decline and increasingly under threat. All trade in wild African apes has been banned on the grounds that they are endangered species, but poaching continues. Deforestation caused by slash-and-burn agriculture, fuel wood collections, and logging also encroaches on the animals' environment and endangers their future. If these magnificent forests continue to be cut and cleared, gorillas, chimpanzees, and bonobos will be faced with extinction.

AN EVIL WIND

The Goma region has trouble enough, what with armed rebellions and the loss of tourist income, but Mother Nature has added some wickedness of her own—a mysterious, invisible killer. Deep beneath Lake Kivu lie large underwater reservoirs of methane and carbon dioxide. Occasionally, some of these poison gases bubble to the surface creating a phenomenon the local people call a mazuku, *which means "evil wind" in Swahili.*

In this seismically active region, the roiling sediment beneath the land can explode in volcanoes, methane explosions, and unseen clouds of poison. Nearly one hundred people die each year from carbon dioxide vents along Lake Kivu's northern shore. People swimming in Kivu often report feeling breathless and lightheaded, which might explain many of the drownings in the lake. Locals report that people are sometimes even swallowed up by random gas bubbles. (Just to add the beautiful lake's evil mystique, the National Geographic Society says lightning strikes Kivu more often than any other place on earth.) Scientists are increasingly worried that a buildup of gases could literally cause the lake to explode—a rare but not unheard of phenomenon.

There might, however, be a silver lining to the lake's unusual chemistry. If the gases, particularly methane, could be extracted and used to produce energy, it could greatly benefit the countries of the African Great Lakes region, particularly Congo and Rwanda. It might also reduce the amount of methane in the lake, lowering the possibility of explosion. Kivu's first large-scale gas-to-power plant went online in Rwanda in May 2016.

the most amazing are those on the Rwenzori Mountains. There giant heather plants grow as high as 15 feet (4.6 m) compared with those 2 feet (0.6 m) high elsewhere; blue-flowering lobelia plants shoot up 10 feet (3 m) above a vivid green carpet of moss.

The many rivers teem with fish, and the coastal waters boast whales and dolphins. Reptiles include pythons in the forests, cobras and other snakes almost everywhere else, and the expected chameleons and lizards.

INTERNET LINKS

http://www.awf.org/wildlife-conservation/bonobo
The African Wildlife Foundation keeps track of the state of bonobos in today's DRC.

https://www.britannica.com/place/Democratic-Republic -of-the-Congo
This site provides a good overview of the Congo's land and climate, with several maps.

http://ngm.nationalgeographic.com/2015/10/congo-river /draper-text
A fascinating journey by barge down the Congo River is the subject of this narrative.

https://www.nytimes.com/2017/08/18/opinion/joseph-conrad -congo-river.html?_r=0
This article is about an excursion down the Congo River, and the way people live on it.

https://www.theguardian.com/cities/2015/feb/10/where-concorde -once-flew-the-story-of-president-mobutus-african-versailles
This enthralling look at Gbadolite is accompanied by a number of eye-opening photos.

HISTORY

An illustration of a suspension bridge across the Itari River in the Congo, from Henry M. Stanley's book *In Darkest Africa* (1890).

THERE WAS A TIME WHEN EUROPE and the rest of the world knew little about the interior of the African continent. Dense equatorial jungle prevented outside explorers from discovering the riches the continent held. European explorers preferred to sail around the continent rather than hack their way into the interior. In many ways, those might have been better times for the African people.

Eventually, Europeans discovered Africa's hidden treasures—ivory, gold, diamonds, emeralds, copper—and not least, the people themselves. From the transatlantic slave trade in the sixteenth century to the colonial domination of the nineteenth and twentieth centuries, European intervention has left behind a rotten legacy. Much of today's poverty, violence, corruption, brutal autocratic dictators, and seemingly never-ending wars, can be traced back to European imperialism and exploitation. The history of Africa—and certainly that of the Congo—has not been a happy one.

THE KONGO KINGDOM

Legends tell of a great and glorious Congolese empire ruled by the Lunda emperor Mwata Yamvo. Those who claim descent from the Lunda today consider themselves of noble ancestry. During the period referred to by European historians as the Middle Ages, the greatest of the Central African kingdoms were the Kongo, which encompassed the lower river basin (today western DRC and northeastern Angola), and the kingdom of the copper-working Luba people in the grasslands of Katanga.

Portuguese sailors greet the king of the Congo in this 1598 engraving.

FIRST EUROPEAN EXPLORERS

In 1482 the Portuguese navigator Diogo Cão explored the estuary of the Congo River and named it Rio de Padrão. He made contact with the Kongo kingdom in order to include it in Portugal's widening empire. Initially the intent was to encourage trade and introduce missionaries. The *mwenekongo* (manikongo), or king, accepted the Portuguese warmly, converted to Christianity, and even agreed to send his son to school in Lisbon. But an increasing demand for slaves began to dominate the relationship with Portugal.

When the mwenekongo had insufficient numbers of captured enemies or local criminals for slaves, the Portuguese sent raiding parties inland, using the Atlantic island of São Tomé as their base. Finding their kingdom shattered, the Kongo people retaliated. The Portuguese moved their base south to Luanda in Angola and sent troops against the Kongo. As would happen too often in African history, European firepower crushed all opposition.

During the seventeenth and eighteenth centuries, the growing slave trade weakened this Central African region drastically. However, the Luba people and, farther south, the Lunda people became rich on iron and copper working. Other small kingdoms grew up in the east, near the Rift Valley lakes, and traded in local goods in addition to slaves. In return the Zanzibar slave

SLAVERY

It is estimated that in the sixteenth century alone, some sixty thousand people were enslaved and shipped out of the Kongo kingdom. The depopulating of Africa to provide for the slave markets of Europe and the Americas continued for another few hundred years. As Africa became regarded as a source of slaves, Africans became devalued as people. Their European overlords felt that they were bringing "civilization" to Africa. African cultures were ignored and crushed. It is hardly surprising that after independence in 1960, one of the first things Congolese in Kinshasa did was to pull down the statue of King Léopold II.

raiders brought with them luxuries such as candles, matches, and furniture such as beds and coffee tables. So despite the depopulating effect of the slave trade, the Central African kingdoms did grow. In 1906 a German explorer, Leo Frobenius, was surprised to find towns with impressively decorated houses, avenues lined with palm trees, and people dressed in velvet and silk with well-wrought metal weapons.

In 1871 the journalist Henry Stanley achieved fame by finding Dr. David Livingstone, who was thought to be lost in the middle of Africa. Three years later Stanley returned as an explorer and was the first European to trace the main course of the Congo River. Earlier explorers had guessed that the source of the Congo was the same lake that fed the Nile. But in 1867 Stanley was the first explorer to chart the main stream. He traveled downstream for more than 1,600 miles (2,575 km), losing many of his men to sickness and starvation, hostile inhabitants, and wild animals, but he showed that above the rapids of the lower Congo was a vast system of navigable inland waterways. Once people realized the river was navigable, it became a main route into Central Africa. But it was never an easy way to travel.

At this time the European nations were looking for a foothold in Africa. King Léopold II of Belgium hired Stanley to create inland communications for what he now claimed as his kingdom. Roads and railways could bypass the rapids and waterfalls on the river system. The scramble for African territories began.

A monument to King Léopold II.

The French tried to prevent Belgian expansion in 1880 by sending Pierre de Brazza to claim the neighboring territory north of the Congo. This became Congo-Brazzaville and is now the Republic of the Congo. Today the capital of the Congo, Brazzaville, and the capital of the DRC, Kinshasa, are separated only by the Congo River. All embassies have their own private boats, and when there are no hostilities between the two countries, diplomats spend much of their time on the river.

BELGIAN COLONIALISM

During the Berlin Conference of 1884—1885, the Congo Free State, which includes what is now the DRC, was awarded to King Léopold II of Belgium. There was nothing "free" about its ownership; Léopold treated the country as his own private property.

Africans were considered uncivilized and had no legal right to own land. They were duty-bound to hand over the produce of the land they worked to the owners. Every village was ordered to provide four people a year to work as full-time slaves for the Congo Free State. These unpaid workers were sent out into the jungle to bring back rubber latex while their wives and children were held as hostages. Some had a hand cut off as punishment for not achieving their quota. Gang bosses actually produced baskets of smoked human hands to prove that they were doing their job properly.

Land and mineral rights were granted to companies that would build roads and railways. Men were chained together to provide the labor required. Léopold robbed the wealth of the land and put it in his own bank account. He used much of the money to build ostentatious palaces and public buildings in Belgium and some to bribe journalists not to report on the situation. Missionaries who were trying to bring a little peace and education to the Congolese were horrified. Reports of the atrocities so embarrassed the Belgian government that it persuaded the king to hand over the governing of the country, which became the Belgian Congo in 1908.

For the next fifty years, the Congolese experienced a more relaxed Belgian rule, which continued to reap material profits from the country but was not so brutal. The colonial attitude toward Africans was well expressed in 1921 by Dr. Albert Schweitzer, who said, "I am your brother, it is true, but your elder brother."

INDEPENDENCE

In 1958 France allowed Congo-Brazzaville to become self-governing. In the Belgian Congo, political parties had been allowed just three years earlier. Rioting in Léopoldville, the capital forced Belgium to send troops in increasing numbers but without much effect. So, reluctantly, independence was granted on June 30, 1960—without sufficient planning or infrastructure in place to give the newly independent nation some semblance of a chance to succeed. The hurriedly arranged election was won by the party headed by Patrice Lumumba (1925—1961), who became prime minister. After considerable disagreement, Joseph Kasavubu (1910—1965), Lumumba's closest rival, was named president.

Six days later, during general unrest caused by political parties unrepresented in the new power structure, the army mutinied over a pay dispute. Violence broke out between black and white civilians, and Belgian troops rushed in to protect the fleeing white people. Five days after that, the province of Katanga seceded. It was soon joined by neighboring Kasai.

Patrice Lumumba, the DRC's first prime minister, in 1960.

THE CONGO CRISIS

The DRC statesman Joseph Kasavubu, shown here in December 1959, would become the country's first president in June 1960.

The new government would not accept Katanga's independence, since Katanga controlled the hugely profitable copper industry. Katanga Province appealed to Belgium for military aid, and civil war broke out. Lumumba asked for help from the United Nations, and peacekeeping forces were sent. However, the UN refused to let the troops help the new Congolese government fight the secessionists, so Prime Minister Lumumba asked for assistance from the Soviet Union. The Soviets sent military advisors and other support.

On September 5, 1960, Kasavubu promptly dismissed Lumumba from office. Lumumba declared Kasavubu's action unconstitutional, and a crisis between the two leaders developed. Lumumba had previously appointed Joseph Mobutu (1930—1997) chief of staff of the new Congo army. Taking advantage of the leadership crisis between Kasavubu and Lumumba, Mobutu garnered enough support within the army to stir up a mutiny. With financial support from the United States and Belgium, Mobutu paid his soldiers privately.

This period, the early 1960s, was the height of the Cold War between the United States and the Soviet Union and their respective allies. A sense of hysteria about the potential spread of communism and leftist ideology—a phenomenon called "the Red Scare"—influenced many US and European political decisions at this time, including the decision to finance Mobutu's quest to attain power in the new state. Mobutu had promised he would resist communist expansion in Africa.

Lumumba, on the other hand, had reached out to the Soviet Union for financial support for his nation not because he was a communist, but because Western countries including the United States had shunned him. It proved to be a fatal error on his part. Thus the series of civil wars and political upheaval that came to be called the Congo Crisis played out as a proxy conflict in the Cold War.

On January 17, 1961, Katangan forces and Belgian officers, supported by foreign interests intent on copper and diamond mines in Katanga and South Kasai, kidnapped and executed Patrice Lumumba. He was thirty-five years old and had served his country as prime minister for little more than two months.

MOBUTU'S RULE

After the UN troops left, the governing coalition led by Moïse Tshombe was defeated by Kasavubu, who once again installed himself as president, supported by Mobutu. In 1965 Mobutu launched a second coup, with the support of the US Central Intelligence Agency (CIA), and made himself head of state. By declaring that he was an enemy of communism, Mobutu ensured that the United States (through the CIA) was firmly on his side.

In due course, Mobutu started a program of Africanization to wipe out vestiges of colonialism. He changed his own name, to Mobutu Sese Seko; ordered his people to replace Christian names with African ones; and altered any place names that he considered a link with colonialism. Thus did Léopoldville become Kinshasa in 1966, and Stanleyville became Kisangani. The country itself was renamed Zaire in 1971.

As long as copper prices remained high, the economy of Zaire was stable. Mobutu gave more power to those local chiefs he counted as his friends and began a systematic milking of the country's wealth. So began the transition to dictatorship that would characterize Mobutu's reign.

In 1977 Katangan rebels living in Angola invaded Katanga Province, captured the mining town of Kolwezi, and massacred European workers and missionaries. Mobutu's army was clearly reluctant to fight, so the area was recaptured with the aid of Moroccan and Belgian mercenaries, with the United States providing aircraft.

When copper prices plunged in the 1970s, the country found itself badly in debt, with high unemployment and increasing inflation. By the 1980s, Zaire was bankrupt. Foreign countries kept providing support and military aid, apparently because Mobutu promised to prevent Soviet expansion in Central Africa.

Anti-Mobutu sympathizers were beaten, jailed, or killed. When even his foreign friends started to object to his dictatorial rule and the suppression of human rights, Mobutu finally allowed opposition parties to be formed in 1990.

Mobutu indulged in reckless extravagance. In the late 1980s, when diplomats, businessmen, and journalists were invited to a luncheon banquet in his palace in Gbadolite, French champagne was offered along with Belgian delicacies flown in that morning and served on gold plates. At the same time, he neglected to pay the army, which threatened to mutiny. Eventually, in 1991, the frustrated army started a wave of widespread looting.

A two-day spree of wanton destruction was called the *pillage* (pee-YAHJ), French for "looting." People began to talk of life before and after the pillage. To find cash to pay the troops, Mobutu doubled the bus fares. In retaliation, the public burned all the buses. The soldiers remained unpaid. Armed and angry, they lost control. Civilians, just as frustrated by low wages, joined in. Mines were looted, stores destroyed, shops and factories burned, hotels wrecked, and trains vandalized. All hope of any economic recovery in Zaire

Kinshasa residents view the damage in the aftermath of the 1991 army riots and looting.

The boy from the Ngbandi ethnic group who grew up in the jungle village of Gbadolite and was christened Joseph Désiré Mobutu died in exile in Morocco on September 7, 1997, as one of the richest ex-presidents in the world. He had renamed his country, its main cities, its main river, and himself. His chosen new name was Mobutu Sese Seko Kuku Ngbenduwaza Banga, which (according to a government-authorized translation) meant "the all-powerful warrior who, because of his endurance and inflexible will to win, will go from conquest to conquest leaving fire in his wake." It was a praise name, a type of African honorific.

Mobutu's father was a domestic cook. After attending a Catholic primary school, Mobutu won a place at the missionary high school in Coquilhatville (now Mbandaka), where he was first in his class. But he was expelled for going to Léopoldville (Kinshasa), which was strictly out of bounds and considered by the missionaries to be a sinful city. As part of his punishment, he was also sentenced to six months in prison and then to seven years in the army. He served first as a pay clerk before being assigned to military headquarters in Léopoldville, where he rose to the rank of sergeant major. In 1956 he was allowed to leave the army. Always a keen reader, he decided to become a journalist and in due course became an editor of Actualités Africaines, *the first weekly paper written "for Congolese by Congolese."*

In the course of his work he met Patrice Lumumba in 1957, when the country was preparing for its first municipal election. Bitter at the constraints of colonial rule, Mobutu went to Brussels to argue successfully for the release of his friend Lumumba, who had been imprisoned by Belgian authorities in the Congo as a disruptive politician. After Lumumba's party won the 1960 election, he rewarded Mobutu with a post as colonel in the army. The arrival of the UN forces aggravated an already confused military situation, which allowed Mobutu to build up his own private army. When a political struggle exploded in September 1960 between Lumumba and Joseph Kasavubu, Mobutu took over the government in a military coup but soon reinstated Kasavubu as president.

Rwandan refugees, fleeing genocidal violence in their homeland, are trying to get to Goma in Zaire (today's DRC).

disappeared into smoke. The result was 80 percent unemployment and a complete breakdown in the financial system.

The notion of looting stayed in people's minds. On several occasions, throughout the country, it happened again. Houses belonging to Europeans were a favorite target. The looters took anything, convinced that if it came from a European house it must be valuable.

THE FIRST CONGO WAR

To understand what happened in Zaire in the mid-1990s, one must look to the Great Lakes region in the east and the small countries of Rwanda and Burundi, which are surrounded by the DRC and Tanzania.

A civil war in Rwanda, which began in 1990, erupted into a shocking mass slaughter of the ethnic Tutsi people that came to be called the Rwandan Genocide. From April to July 1994, between 500,000 and one million Tutsi were murdered by the Rwandan Hutu-controlled government. In response, the heavily-armed, pro-Tutsi Rwandan Patriotic Front overthrew the government and took over the country. This sent some two million Rwandans, mostly Hutu, fleeing the country. The refugees poured over Congo's eastern border, settling into camps mostly around the city of Goma. The camps served as de facto army bases for the militant Hutu who had carried out the genocide, and this caused tremendous tension with the local Banyamulenge, who are primarily of the Tutsi ethnicity.

ENTER KABILA

Aware that the Hutu were planning to use their lands as a launching pad for attacks on Rwanda, the Banyamulenge became rebels. They went on the offensive against both the Hutu militia and the Zairean army. They bombarded a Hutu refugee camp with rockets, mortars, and heavy artillery. In panic 700,000 refugees started heading back toward Rwanda.

Meanwhile, in Congo, opposition to Mobutu was rising, and long-time Marxist revolutionary Laurent Kabila (1939—2001), living in exile, was ready to take advantage of the upheaval. He rallied forces in eastern Congo, and Rwandan and Ugandan armies backing Kabila (1939—2001) invaded the Congo. The combined effort was called the Alliance of Democratic Forces for the Liberation of Congo-Zaire, or AFDL.

By November 1996, they had seized the towns of Goma and Bukavu. They were supported by Rwanda, Burundi, Uganda, and Zambia. Although the rebel leader Laurent Kabila later insisted that his forces came from many ethnic groups of Zaire, it was in the Great Lakes that it all began.

For seven months, Kabila's growing army surged across the country. The only opposition came from Mobutu's own presidential guard and his foreign mercenaries. Kabila's earliest successes came in the Great Lakes region. In February 1997, his forces took the military garrison town of Kindu, a railway depot on the Congo River. Within a month, the rebels controlled Kisangani after Mobutu's troops abandoned the city.

Mobutu asked South Africa's president, Nelson Mandela, to mediate, but Kabila agreed to talks without agreeing to a cease-fire. Meanwhile, in April, Kabila captured Lubumbashi, key to the mining industry.

In seven months Kabila had captured nearly half of the country. Mandela brought Southern and Central African leaders together in South Africa, and they all agreed that Kabila's success was inevitable. On May 17, 1997, Mobutu's senior generals told him that they could not defend Kinshasa. Mobutu agreed to resign, changed his mind, and then finally left Zaire around midnight.

Kabila subsequently became president and changed the country's name to Democratic Republic of the Congo.

THE SECOND CONGO WAR

The Second Congo War began in August 1998 and officially ended in July 2003, though hostilities continue to this day, mostly in the eastern provinces.

Laurent Kabila (1939–2001) was born on a ranch in Katanga Province, a member of a subtribe of the Luba people. He studied political philosophy at a French university and returned to the Congo to start his political career shortly after the country gained independence from Belgium in 1960.

He was a strong supporter of Patrice Lumumba. After Lumumba was assassinated in 1961, Kabila fled to Tanzania, and from there he mounted attacks into the Congo for ten years. He forged strong ties with President Yoweri Museveni in Uganda and with Paul Kagame, who led the Tutsi rebel army that took power in Rwanda in July 1994.

When Kabila emerged in October 1996 as the leader of a rebel army, he seemed to represent the change that people in Zaire wanted so much. To the surprise of the world, his victorious march across the country was not the bloodbath that had been expected.

Described by a journalist as a mixture of arrogance and ignorance, Kabila was known to his supporters as Mzee, a respectful Swahili term meaning "Grand Old Man." But he turned out to be no better than Mobutu. His policies differed little from Mobutu's and were characterized by corruption and human-rights abuses.

When Kabila gained control of the capital in May 1997, many Congolese saw him as a pawn of foreign powers. On July 28, 1998, he thanked Rwanda for its help and backing in putting him into power and ordered all Rwandan and Ugandan military forces to leave the country. The Banyamulenge were alarmed by this, and on August 2, 1998, the Banyamulenge in the city of Goma erupted into mutiny. A rebel group, the Rally for Congolese Democracy (RCD), backed by Rwanda and Uganda, emerged and occupied a portion of northeastern Congo. Uganda also created and subsequently supported a rebel group, the Movement for the Liberation of Congo (MLC). The governments of

Namibia, Zimbabwe, Angola, Chad, and Sudan supported Kabila, and thus a multi-sided war began.

THE SECOND KABILA

Laurent Kabila died on January 18, 2001, following an assassination attempt two days earlier. His son, Joseph Kabila (b. 1971), replaced him as president, and on December 17, 2002, the many warring factions came together and signed a Global and All-Inclusive Agreement, which made provisions to set up a transitional government. The transitional government came into being on July 18, 2003, but the warring parties refused to give up power to a centralized and neutral national administration. A high level of official corruption caused further instability in this long-suffering nation. On July 30, 2006, the first free elections in four decades took place, and a second round between Joseph Kabila and former MLC rebel leader Jean-Pierre Bemba was held on October 29, 2006. Joseph Kabila was officially inaugurated as president on December 6, 2006.

DRC President Joseph Kabila speaks to the UN General Assembly in New York in 2010.

In 2011, he was re-elected for a second term, though his opponent Ètienne Tshisekedi—as well as neutral international observers—openly disputed the results. Kabila's second term expired in December 2016, according to the DRC constitution. However, as of this writing in early 2018, despite various stalling tactics and promises, he has refused to step down. The president, meanwhile, has become extremely unpopular. For one thing, he has been widely accused of looting millions of dollars in public assets.

Protests against the government—and against Kabila in particular—have left scores of people dead. For example, in December 2017, at least eight people were killed and a dozen altar boys were arrested in the country after security forces cracked down on planned church protests against Kabila's refusal to leave office. Catholic churches, and some Protestant ones as well, had called for a peaceful march to protest a delay in elections and Kabila's unconstitutional intent to stay in office. In response, Kabila's government

In 2010, the well-known Congolese human rights activist, Floribert Chebeya, was found murdered. Chebeya, who headed the humanitarian organization Voice of the Voiceless, had spent years compiling data on political oppression, incarcerations, torture, and deaths under the repressive DRC government. His body was discovered shortly after he had been summoned to meet with the country's inspector general of police at police headquarters in Kinshasa. The cause of death was never released.

Chebeya's murder was met with international outrage and mourning. The UN, the European Union, the United States and numerous countries, and some fifty international rights organizations called for an investigation. A year later, five police officers—three of them in absentia, as they had fled—were convicted of the murder. President Joseph Kabila was implicated in ordering the murder, but never charged.

also issued an order to shut down all text messaging and internet services indefinitely across the DRC for what it called "reasons of state security."

NEVER-ENDING WAR

It may be inaccurate to claim the Second Congo War ever stopped. In fact, it has been dubbed "Africa's world war" because it has been the deadliest conflict since World War II. And also, at the height of the hostilities, nine countries were fighting each other on the soil of the DRC. This seemingly never-ending war has so far claimed up to six million lives, either as a direct result of fighting or because of disease and malnutrition.

Some of the neighboring countries involved in the conflict, such as Rwanda and Uganda, have been accused of deliberately prolonging the war by funding rebel groups. The chaos and anarchy allows them to covertly plunder the Congo's natural resources.

In fact, the country's inherent wealth—copper, gold, diamonds, uranium, oil, and other highly valued resources—might well be the reason, or a good part of it, for the ongoing violence. According to some analysts, as long as the DRC government fails to function legally, then corrupt ruling officials and their criminal business networks can siphon off the country's treasure, make profits and hold onto power. A 2010 UN report says criminal networks within the DRC army promote violence in order to profit from mining, smuggling, and poaching. As in the days of King Léopold II's very similar venture, violence works to keep the system running. Until it doesn't.

However, the situation is so complex that even that is a simplistic explanation. As the Democratic Republic of the Congo teeters on the edge of complete meltdown, the world watches in horror and dread.

INTERNET LINKS

http://www.bbc.com/news/world-africa-13286306
The BBC offers a timeline of key events in the history of the DRC.

**https://enoughproject.org/blog/congo-colonialism-through
-dictatorship-1400s-1997**
This organization, which works for peace in Africa, presents a quick overview of Congolese history.

**https://www.theatlantic.com/international/archive/2013/06/the
-origins-of-war-in-the-drc/277131**
This article examines the ongoing wars in eastern DRC.

**https://www.uneca.org/publications/conflicts-democratic-republic
-congo-causes-impact-and-implications-great-lakes-region**
This page links to a PDF of the 2015 UN Economic Commission for Africa report on the conflicts in the DRC.

GOVERNMENT

A large sign displays President Joseph Kabila's image outside the government building in Kinshasa.

3

A FRICAN TRIBES TRADITIONALLY HAD a chief they could look up to. He had to be powerful enough to help them and to solve problems. No chief would surrender power voluntarily. If he was a rogue, he had to be a highly successful one, skillful enough to defeat any rivals. In return for his skill and leadership, his people would show respect and present him with gifts of money or produce.

Of course those in authority were going to be richer than the people they governed. What was not acceptable was a chief ignoring his people and allowing them to go hungry.

THE COLONIAL INHERITANCE

The Congo Free State was founded by the Belgians in 1885 and was governed first as a private kingdom for King Léopold II, and from 1908 to 1960 as a Belgian colony. In those days a white man had an air of authority that was respected, even feared, by the Congolese. "A beard on the face is a sign of power," they would say. The Belgians ruled and legislated not for the good or happiness of the inhabitants but for their own profit. They enslaved much of the population, made them work for the advantage of Belgium, and took the profits home. In doing so

"In a word, everything is for sale, anything can be bought in our country. ... If you want to steal, steal a little in a nice way. But if you steal too much to become rich overnight, you'll be caught."
—President Mobutu Sese Seko in 1977.

they set up an administrative framework of local governors and courts to hear local grievances. They also built a good network of roads and the beginning of a railroad system.

CONGOLESE POLITICS

As the tide of world opinion turned toward encouraging African independence, the Belgians appointed the first Congolese as members of the governor-general's advisory council in 1947 but gave them a limited role. These first Congolese politicians learned some political skills through their association with the trade unions.

Crowds of Congolese people celebrate independence in Léopoldville.

Patrice Lumumba was one of those who started the first fraternal associations for workers, called *amicales* (AM-ee-KAHL), in the mid-1950s. Then, in October 1958, he formed the Mouvement National Congolais (MNC), with a public declaration that "independence is not a gift to be given by Belgium, but a fundamental right of the Congolese people." When this surge of independent thought led to riots, the MNC was dissolved, and its leaders were imprisoned. But Belgium did agree to hold elections, which would be followed by its withdrawal from the colony.

Trying to make up for its years of inaction, the colonial administration appointed seven hundred Africans to senior civil-service posts, which previously had been reserved for Europeans. In 1959 Belgium passed a tough law against racial segregation.

Independence was declared on June 30, 1960, together with the first constitution and the establishment of six autonomous provincial governments. In the first national election, the MNC won a majority, and Lumumba was elected prime minister. But the excitement was wrecked by violence as the Congolese army mutinied against its white officers, completing the collapse of the colonial administration.

Taking advantage of the state of turmoil, Congolese businessman Moïse Tshombe declared independence for Katanga on July 11, with himself as president; and southern Kasai declared independence one month later. The Christian, anti-communist, pro-Western Tshombe declared, "We are seceding from chaos." He demanded the UN recognize independent Katanga and asked the Belgian government to send military officers to recruit and train a Katangese army. Lumumba, meanwhile, enlisted the help of UN troops.

President Joseph Kasavubu dismissed Prime Minister Lumumba, who in turn declared the president deposed. The army tried to "neutralize" both men but soon showed itself as the ally of Kasavubu. Lumumba was held under house arrest; he escaped but was recaptured and sent to Katanga, where he and two of his colleagues were murdered.

In 1961 UN forces ended Russian technical aid to the country, causing considerable tension between the United States and the Soviet Union. Then the UN's secretary-general, Dag Hammarskjöld, was killed in a plane crash while trying to bring about a cease-fire in the civil war. Into this political uncertainty came General Joseph Mobutu. Tshombe succumbed to UN pressure and agreed to return Katanga to the Congo in January 1963.

POLITICAL STRUGGLES

One of Mobutu's long-standing political opponents was Étienne Tshisekedi, imprisoned in 1980 for publishing a fifty-two page letter condemning dictatorship. When the country's multiparty system was introduced in 1990, Tshisekedi was chosen prime minister. Mobutu dismissed him and did so on two more occasions when parliament appointed Tshisekedi as prime minister.

Another opponent was Laurent Monsengwo, the Catholic archbishop of Kisangani. In 1992 he gathered together a grand council of Mobutu's opponents, and together they worked for four years to draft a plan for the transition to democracy.

Mobutu's final opponent was, of course, Laurent Kabila. His opposition crystallized in October 1996 with the alliance of four groups called Alliance des Forces Démocratiques pour la Libération du Congo-Kinshan (Coalition of Democratic Forces for the Liberation of Congo-Kinshasa), or AFDL; his own Popular Revolutionary Party; the National Council of Resistance for Democracy; the Revolutionary Movement for the Liberation of Zaire, led by

One of the words coined by the international press was Mobutism, signifying the highly African-slanted viewpoint of the Zairean president. Another word that was often used to describe his form of government was kleptocracy, to describe state-sponsored corruption. And despite Mobutu's Africanization of place names, he did little to Africanize his government, which exploited the opportunity for corruption. The colonial structures stayed in place, and self-interest—his—was the norm.

Although he has been gone now for more than a decade, Mobuto still figures mightily in Congo, as he sucked billions of dollars of wealth out of the country, leaving it impoverished. He also set the tone for African leadership that author Philip Gourevitch calls "monomaniacal, perfectly corrupt, and absolutely ruinous to his nation." In 2011, TIME magazine described Mobutu as the "archetypal African dictator."

Mobutu developed his absolute power by intimidation and unpredictability in his actions. Security and intelligence were essential elements of Mobutism. The president used several intelligence agencies to keep him constantly informed about anyone expressing dissent or posing any sort of threat to the system. It was dangerous to speak Mobutu's name or write it in case the secret police were too close. People cautiously referred to him as "Uncle Mo." Mobutu maintained his own Israeli-trained presidential guard of ten thousand men. One group of them became known as les hiboux (layz EE-boo), or "the owls," since they worked mostly by night, serving as a death squad to maintain the power of the president.

No civil servant bothered to provide service unless he was bribed to do so. Government ministers required payoffs for construction projects, teachers wanted payoffs from their students, and policemen halted motorists and gave them a choice between a payoff and arrest. This was kleptocracy. Like a universal tax, though invisible, it was known and expected by all.

Masusu Nindaga; and the People's Democratic Alliance, led by Deo Bugera.

Following Laurent Kabila's death, his son, Joseph Kabila, continued with the transitional parliament his father had set up. He then went on to win two consecutive presidential terms, in 2006 and 2011. At the end of his second term, however, he refused to step down and the country did not hold elections in 2016 as required by the constitution.

THE CONSTITUTION

The DRC is now under the Constitution of the Third Republic. A constitutional referendum was held in December 2005, and 84 percent of the voters approved of the constitution. The constitution establishes a decentralized, semi-presidential republic with a separation of powers among the three branches of government—executive, legislative, and judiciary—and a division of authority between the central government and twenty-six semiautonomous provinces drawn along ethnic and cultural lines.

PARLIAMENTARY GOVERNMENT

The president is the head of state, and is elected by a simple majority for up to two consecutive five-year terms. The last election was held on November 28, 2011. The expected 2016 elections have been pushed back to an

Voters wait on line in December 2005 in the Bandal district of Kinshasa, with their electoral cards in hand.

A CONSTITUTIONAL PREAMBLE, or introduction, states a government's principals and purposes. It establishes the source of the government's authority and sets the tone of its ideals. In this preamble (only part of it is printed here), note the implied references to the injustices of the past regime (Mobutu); and the commitment, going forward, to human rights. Despite the lofty goals set down here, the very first president to serve under this constitution, Joseph Kabila, has already deviated from it by refusing to leave office at the end of his term.

PREAMBLE

We, the Congolese People,

United by destiny and history around the noble ideas of liberty, fraternity, solidarity, justice, peace and work;

Driven by our common will to build in the heart of Africa a State under the rule of law and a powerful and prosperous Nation based on a real political, economic, social and cultural democracy;

Considering that injustice and its corollaries, impunity, nepotism, regionalism, tribalism, clan rule and patronage are, due to their manifold vices, at the origin of the general decline of values and the ruin of the country;

Affirming our determination to safeguard and consolidate national independence and unity by respecting our positive diversities and particularities;

Reaffirming our adherence and attachment to the Universal Declaration of Human Rights, the African Charter on Human and Peoples' Rights, the United Nations Conventions on the Rights of the Child and the Rights of Women, particularly to the goal of equal representation of men and women in the institutions of the country, as well as to the international instruments relating to the protection and promotion of human rights …

Declare to solemnly adopt this Constitution.

uncertain date in 2018. The cabinet, or ministers of state, are appointed by the president. He also appoints the prime minister, who is the head of the government.

The parliament has two branches: the National Assembly, with 500 seats; and the Senate, with 108 seats. Members of the National Assembly, the lower but more powerful house, are elected by direct vote, are called national deputies and serve five-year terms. Senators are indirectly elected by the legislatures of the twenty-six provinces, and also serve for five years.

At the province level, each provincial assembly elects a governor, and the governor, with up to ten ministers, is in charge of the provincial executive branch. The majority of the domains of power are still vested in the central government, and the governor is responsible to the provincial assembly.

THE JUDICIARY

The Congolese legal system is primarily based on Belgian law, but includes elements of customary or tribal law. Local customary laws regulate both personal status laws—like marriage and divorce laws—and property rights, which primarily focus on the inheritance and land tenure systems. One distinctive characteristic of customary laws is that they do not have general application across the country but only apply to the traditional communities from which they originate. Even though the Constitution places customary laws below state laws, customary laws are said to settle 75 percent of disputes in the Congo.

The 2006 constitution essentially rebuilds the judiciary from scratch. Previously, the DRC's judicial system had had little investment during the past decade. Most of the courts were nonfunctional; their personnel having gone unpaid for years. Magistrates were badly trained and unsupported. Mismanagement or corruption often characterized judgments made, sometimes fueling community grievances and furthering conflict.

The general population still lacks confidence in the judiciary. It is estimated that only a very small percentage of disputes end up in courts of law, not because parties to the disputes have better options but because they are so suspicious of the judiciary that they prefer other means, including the

FARDC members patrol an area of rebel activity in North Kivu in January 2018.

police, security services, the military, or in rural areas, the traditional or tribal arbitration mentioned above.

The new constitution provides for an independent judiciary consisting of the Court of Cassation, with twenty-six justices; the Constitutional Court, with nine judges; the Council of State (a federal administrative court), the Military High Court, and lower courts and tribunals throughout the country. The government is working on building this judicial arm accordingly.

THE ARMED FORCES

Tthe DRC military is the Forces Armées de la République Démocratique du Congo (FARDC), or Armed Forces of the Democratic Republic of the Congo. Officially, it is made up of primarily land forces, a small air force, and an even smaller navy. Together the three services number between 144,000 and 159,000 personnel. However, many international observers report that the FARDC is a shambles. It is said to be underfunded, underequipped, corrupt, and top-heavy with former warlords acting as colonels. The air force cannot carry out its responsibilities, as few aircraft are capable of being restored to service, and the navy is in total disarray.

Since the end of the Second Congo War, the government has trying to create a reliable, well trained, cohesive national army (the FARDC) out of various regional fighting factions. These former rebel groups and militias—some of which were former rivals—had been largely built along ethnic, political, and regional lines. The veterans of past factional skirmishes and wars have varying loyalties, levels of training, and many have probably taken part in human rights abuses—such as rape, torture, and the murder of civilians—they might once have considered just part of the job.

Adding to the chaos and confusion, numerous outside entities have been brought in to train troops, including the Chinese, Russian, and Belgian governments, a private US contractor, and various other international training organizations. This naturally results in a wide range of standards and procedures and doesn't provide the cohesiveness the Congolese forces need.

President Joseph Kabila also has a presidential force called the Republican Guard, which is more than ten thousand strong. This unit is not a part of FARDC and appears to be better paid and trained. Nevertheless, the guards have been accused of inappropriate behavior on a regular basis, and it's unclear where their true loyalty lies.

The United Nations mission in the DRC currently has some 95,000 peacekeeping troops (United Nations Organization Stabilization Mission in the Democratic Republic of the Congo, or MONUSCO) assisting Congolese authorities in maintaining security. The troops are mainly focused on ethnic conflicts in eastern Congo.

INTERNET LINKS

http://www.bbc.com/news/world-africa-13283212
The BBC country profile includes a profile of the leader, the media, and a history timeline.

https://www.cia.gov/library/publications/the-world-factbook /geos/cg.html
The CIA World Factbook provides up-to-date information about the Congolese government.

http://www.constitutionnet.org/sites/default/files/DRC%20-%20 Congo%20Constitution.pdf
The 2005 version of the DRC constitution can be found here.

https://monusco.unmissions.org/en
This is the English language site of the MONUSCO peacekeeping mission.

ECONOMY

A worker holds a bar of gold at the Kibali gold mine in 2014.

4

HOW CAN IT BE THAT A COUNTRY SO rich in natural resources is, at the same time, so incredibly poor? With vast forests, wonderfully varied biodiversity, fertile soil, excellent hydroelectric potential, and substantial endowments of cobalt, copper, and industrial diamonds, the DRC should be quite a wealthy country. Instead, years of widespread corruption and mismanagement, coupled with ongoing conflicts and wars, have left it one of the world's most impoverished countries.

People survive by cutting back to one meal a day. They buy nothing but essential goods. Worn clothes are mended again and again, old rubber tires are turned into sandals, and cardboard boxes become the walls of makeshift homes. In many places in the Congo, villagers have gone to a barter economy, exchanging produce for what is required. Much of the economic activity that occurs in this informal, "shadow" sector is not reflected in official data, such as the gross domestic product (GDP).

Between 2005 and 2012, the nation's poverty rate decreased from 71 percent to 64 percent. Life expectancy at birth increased from 47.8 years in 2005 to 57.7 years in 2017, while the rate of child mortality decreased by 30 percent, all of which seems to signify good news.

"While $134 billion flows into the continent (of Africa) each year, predominantly in the form of loans, foreign investment, and aid, $192 billion is taken out, mainly in profits made by foreign companies, tax evasion, and the costs of adapting to climate change. The result is that Africa suffers a net loss of $58 billion a year. As such, the idea that we are aiding Africa is flawed; it is Africa that is aiding the rest of the world."

—Health Poverty Action report, July 14, 2014.

Gross domestic product (GDP) is a measure of a country's total production. The number reflects the total value of goods and services produced over one year. Economists use it to determine whether a country's economy is growing or contracting. Growth is good, while a falling GDP means trouble. Dividing the GDP by the number of people in the country determines the GDP per capita (per person). This number provides an indication of a country's average standard of living—the higher the better.

In 2017, the GDP per capita in the Democratic Republic of the Congo was approximately $800. That was the third worst in the world, number 228 out of 230 countries. (For comparison, the GDP per capita in the United States for that year was $57,400, and even that was ranked twentieth in the world.)

However, the DRC still ranks a very low 176 out of 187 countries, on the 2016 Human Development Index (HDI). Calculated by the UN, this is not only an economic ranking. It's a composite measurement of a country's average achievement in three basic dimensions of human development: a long and healthy life, knowledge, and a decent standard of living.

At the time of its independence in 1960, the Democratic Republic of the Congo was the second most industrialized country in Africa after South Africa. So what happened?

AGRICULTURE AND FOOD

At independence the Belgian Congo left an inheritance of plantation agriculture with a few African-style cattle ranches situated in the higher regions of the country, which are free of tsetse flies. For a while the country continued producing enough to feed itself. Then during the 1970s many of the foreign-owned plantations and ranches were nationalized. Production dropped to a point where up to half of the food supplies had to be imported from South Africa.

Once an exporter of food, the DRC now grows too little to meet even the basic food needs of its 83 million people. Some 60 percent of the active population has to undertake some form of subsistence farming to meet their basic food needs. Subsistence food crops in tropical areas principally consist of cassava, corn, tubers, and sorghum. Most of the commercial crops such as coffee, cocoa, rubber, tea, palm oil, and sugarcane are grown on plantations, with the production of tobacco and cotton largely in the hands of private small-hold farmers. In addition, agriculture has suffered from the notorious decay of the transportation infrastructure, in particular the road networks, through which produce is distributed around the country.

There are small numbers of goats, pigs, and sheep but hardly any serious livestock farming. Scrawny chickens form the main source of meat. Fish could be a valuable source of food, but this is another underexploited sector with huge potential.

Two men carry cabbages to sell in Goma, the capital city of the North Kivu province bordering Rwanda.

MINING AND INDUSTRY

Beneath the surface, the land in the Congo holds treasures, particularly in the Katanga province. The country has an estimated 28 percent of the world's cobalt, as well as reserves of petroleum, copper, manganese, silver, gold, and industrial-grade diamonds. There are also reserves of zinc, bauxite, tin, and iron that are almost untapped. DRC has the world's largest reserved of coltan, a black metallic ore used in the manufacture of electronic products, but the mining of this mineral is deeply wrapped up in the region's conflicts. Outbreaks of violence deter foreign investment and have displaced hundreds of thousands of workers.

In the days of the Belgian Congo, there was no attempt at diversification. Copper seemed a satisfactory way of becoming rich, so most efforts were centered on that one mining industry, though it was uranium from Lubumbashi that helped create the atomic bomb that destroyed Hiroshima in 1945.

Some improvements were gradually made. Roads and railways were built, and new construction saw European-style architecture rise in the

Men dig for diamonds in a muddy pit near the city of Mbuji-Mayi in south-central Congo.

cities. The Inga Dam on the lower Congo was constructed to provide hydroelectric power, and there was an increasing appreciation of the mineral wealth in the ground. In the years after independence, copper prices stayed high; during 1973 they doubled.

When President Mobutu launched his Africanization program, he removed a large number of skilled foreigners from important business positions. Then in 1975 the international price of copper collapsed. With it went any hope of rescuing the country's economy—all the financial eggs had been in one basket. The country's copper output plunged from 476,000 tons (483,638 metric tons) in 1986 to about 31,000 tons (31,497 metric tons) in 1994.

Since 1994, diamonds have become the country's leading export, following the decline in the production of copper; more than 10 percent of export earnings now come from diamond production, and the DRC produces about 90 percent of the world's small industrial diamonds. Most diamond mining is done by hand, a process called artisanal or small-scale mining. This sector is largely unregulated and has high instances of child labor. Conditions are brutal and dangerous. Rebel groups often loot the mines and use the minerals to finance their war operations, in transactions that are never recorded officially.

TRANSPORTATION

Trying to get around in the Congo has always been difficult. The terrain and climate of the vast country present serious barriers to road and rail construction. There are no contiguous highways or railroads that traverse the country, so traveling is a matter of cobbling together shorter spurts along extremely rough dirt roads and rivers. Trains, for the most part, are notoriously unreliable. Chronic economic mismanagement and internal conflict led to serious underinvestment in infrastructure over many years.

Water transport on the country's 9,321 miles (15,000 km) of navigable rivers and connected lakes is the main way to get from one place to another. Most of the old, state-owned riverboats sit rusting, but privately owned barges and other makeshift vessels move thousands of passengers and untold amounts of freight each year.

There is an international airport in Kinshasa, and there are reasonably good airports at Kisangani, Lubumbashi, and Goma. Congo's last national airline, Air Zaire, went bankrupt in the 1990s, and all air carriers certified by the DRC had been banned from European Union airports by the European Commission because of inadequate safety standards. In 2015, the new Congo Airways launched with promises of improved safety and maintenance. With its fleet of five commercial jet aircraft, the company serves nine Congolese destinations from its base at N'djili Airport in Kinshasa.

People cram into the back of a van traveling through Kinshasa.

In 2014 there were 2,490 miles (4,007 km) of railway track reported usable. The national system is operated mostly by the Société Nationale des Chemins de Fer du Congo (SNCC). Not all rail lines link up, but they are generally connected by river transport.

HYDROELECTRIC POWER

With its system of mighty rivers, and their abundant rapids, the DRC's hydroelectric potential is enormous. Theoretically, the country could produce 13 percent of the world's capacity and 50 percent of Africa's. And yet, the DRC makes use of just 2 percent of this potential. Only 9 percent of the total population has electricity, mostly in the urban areas. Rural parts of the country are almost entirely without access to it, and what little power is there is extremely expensive. A lack of electricity naturally inhibits industrial, agricultural, and technological growth.

THE GRAND INGA DAM

Construction on the world's largest dam has been on the brink of commencing for years. So far, however, the Grand Inga Dam continues to exist only on paper. Should it ever get built, it will have almost twice the capacity of the Three Gorges Dam in China,

which is currently the largest energy-generating body ever constructed.

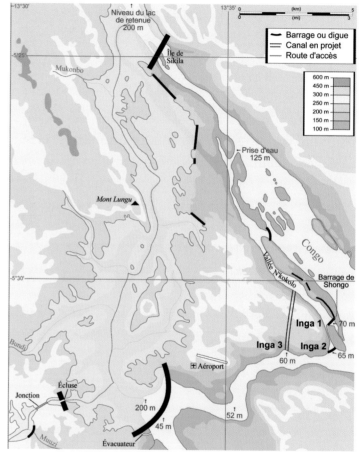

The proposed dam at Inga Falls on the Congo River would join two smaller hydroelectric dams—Inga I and Inga II—as well as the intended Inga III, if that one gets built. Inga Falls is a spectacular group of rapids that are part of the Livingstone Falls system. At Inga, the Congo River drops 315 feet (96 m) over the course of 9 miles (15 km).

On May 2016 it looked as if construction was due to begin within months. But in July 2016, the World Bank withdrew its funding following disagreements over the project. Although the proposed dam is heralded as the answer to many of the problems in the DRC—not to mention all of Africa—critics charge its benefits would bypass the nation's poor people and go directly to the good of huge corporate interests. Not only that, but the country's deeply entrenched corruption shows little sign of abating, which does not augur well for the future of the project.

The heaviest concentration of hydroelectric consumption is in the mining areas and Kinshasa. The hydroelectric dam completed in 1972 on the lower Congo River at Inga Falls began initially to supply 300,000 kilowatts of electricity. After the completion of the second stage in 1982, Inga's capacity rose to 2.3 million kilowatts. The dam has a theoretical potential estimated at 30 million kilowatts. DRC exports electricity to Zambia, Burundi, Congo (Brazzaville), and Angola.

INTERNET LINKS

https://www.africanexponent.com/post/billions-lost-in-profits-by -foreign-companies-tax-evasion-1953
The article "Seven Top Reasons Why Africa Is Still Poor" regards Africa in general, but much of the information applies to the Congo.

http://foreignpolicy.com/2015/05/08/the-river-that-swallows-all -dams-congo-river-inga-dam
This long but readable article provides an in-depth look at the history of the proposed Grand Inga Dam, along with a comprehensive overview of DRC's history and economy.

http://www.new-ag.info/en/country/profile.php?a=641
This site provides an overview of agriculture in the Congo.

http://www.slate.com/articles/news_and_politics/roads/2017/04 /in_the_democratic_republic_of_congo_artisanal_mining_is_a_ remnant_of_the.html
This article takes a gritty look at diamond mining in the DRC.

http://www.worldbank.org/en/country/drc/overview
The World Bank provides a concise, up-to-date overview of the DRC's economic situation.

ENVIRONMENT

A baby hippopotamus huddles close to its mother in Virunga National Park.

5

In 2017, eight park rangers were killed protecting the animals of Virunga National Park from poachers. Over the past twenty years, more than 160 rangers were murdered protecting the park.

VAST EXPANSES OF LAND IN THIS magnificent country are covered by lush rain forests that are home to an amazing range of plants and animals. Many of them, such as the strange and beautiful okapi, are endemic to this region—they exist nowhere else on earth. Five of the Congo's national parks have been listed as World Heritage Sites.

The DRC has the greatest extent of tropical rain forests in Africa, covering more than 331 million acres (134 million hectares)—almost 60 percent of the country. The forests in the eastern sector are amazingly diverse, as they are among the few forest areas in Africa to have survived the Ice Age. About 45 percent of the DRC is covered by primary forest, which provides a refuge for several large mammal species driven to extinction in other African countries. Overall the country is known to have more than 10,000 species of plants, 400 species of mammals, 1,000 species of birds, 300 of reptiles, and 200 of amphibians.

Despite this richness, during the past twenty years the forests have been the site of terrible violence and immense human suffering, which spilled over from Rwanda and other neighboring countries. During the First and Second Congo Wars, fighting and the movement of millions of refugees through forest regions decimated wildlife and took a heavy toll on protected areas.

Poverty-related forest degradation also stems from slash-and-burn agriculture on the part of the increasing rural population, which lacks livelihood alternatives. Political instability has further reduced opportunities for diversification and investment in more productive, sustainable farming. Another threat is the bushmeat trade—the hunting, selling, and eating of African jungle animals—a tradition that continues due to a lack of inexpensive alternative sources of protein. Indiscriminate shooting of livestock by militias has also posed a serious threat, and the mining of minerals causes environmental damage as well. All these activities have led to the pollution and degradation (including desertification) of the soil and to water and soil erosion.

THE ECOSYSTEM

Inside the rain forests are several layers of life, each with its own ecology. On the forest floor, where hardly any sunlight reaches, it is hot, dark, and damp. This level shelters browsing animals, lichens, and fungi, as well as fish and reptiles in the pools. Immediately above ground level is the understory, where many varieties of monkeys swing through the twisting liana creepers. Approximately 100 feet (30 m) above ground is a thick canopy of leaves and branches, home to many varieties of birds. Towering above them are the shoots of the emergents, the new growth reaching toward the sun.

Although these huge trees and the rich stores of plant and animal life may look dense and strong, they are actually fragile. Because each plant and animal is interdependent, the system is quickly damaged by any disturbance. Uncontrolled logging operations do more than just cut down trees; they destroy habitat.

The forested areas are home to elephants, chimpanzees, gorillas, several species of monkeys and baboons, and rare creatures such as the okapi—which looks like a combination of a zebra and a giraffe—and the giant wild boar. In the grasslands, buffalo and antelopes are hunted by lions and leopards, followed by the scavengers: jackals, hyenas, and vultures. The rivers still abound with crocodiles and hippos; both are dangerous to human beings, who leave them well alone.

The beautiful trees in the DRC include species of red cedar, oak, walnut, mahogany, palm, and silk-cotton. Among the native flowers are orchids, lilies, lobelias, and gladioli.

Birds include brightly colored parrots, quaint pelicans, many species of sunbirds, and birds raised or hunted for food: pigeons, ducks, geese, and ubiquitous scrawny chickens. Eagles and hornbills fly over the grasslands. There are insects everywhere. Mosquitoes carry malaria; tsetse flies cause sleeping sickness; midges infest any area that is moist.

ENDANGERED ANIMALS

Hunting for bushmeat and the illegal exotic wildlife trade have had a serious impact on the populations of several forests animals. Habitat destruction by mining, logging, the reliance on fuelwood, and the clearing of forests for agriculture further threaten the primates and other endangered species of the jungle. Primates are at particular risk. Grauer's gorillas (eastern lowland gorilla) are critically endangered; bonobos are threatened, as mentioned earlier; and chimpanzees are in grave peril from the alarming uptick in the commercial bushmeat trade.

The giraffe-like okapi was unknown outside of Africa until 1901.

OKAPI The okapi is a mammal native to the Ituri rain forest, located in the northeast of the DRC. Although the okapi bears striped markings reminiscent of the zebra's, it is most closely related to the giraffe. The body shape is similar to that of the giraffe, except that okapis have much shorter necks. Both species have very long—12 inches (30 cm)—and flexible blue tongues that they use to strip leaves and buds from trees. Okapis are threatened by habitat destruction and poaching. Conservation work in the DRC includes the continuing study of okapi behavior and lifestyle, which led to the creation in 1992 of the Okapi Wildlife Reserve.

FOREST ELEPHANT The forest elephant, a distinct species of African elephant, lives in the forests of West and Central Africa. Despite a near-universal ban on trade in ivory, the demand for it continues, particularly

GORILLAS

There are two species of Eastern Gorillas in Africa and both live in the the the DRC—the Mountain Gorilla (Gorilla beringei beringei) and the Grauer's Gorilla (Gorilla beringei graueri). Mountain gorillas live in forests high in the mountains, as their name implies. One of their last remaining sanctuaries is in the Virunga Mountains. There are only about 880 mountain gorillas left in the wild—a small increase in the population, which is good news—and Virunga National Park provides a home to about half of them. The Virunga

Reserve has been slashed and burned by squatters who turned the terrain into agricultural land, and in a notorious massacre in 2007, ten rare gorillas were shot and killed.

Although their skin and the majority of their body hair are black, the older males develop gray hair on their back, which is why they are called silverbacks. A silverback leads a family group that includes one or two younger males, several females, and their young.

Poaching and war have also threatened populations of the Grauer's gorilla, in the eastern DRC. The International Union for Conservation of Nature (IUCN) Red List of Threatened Species reports the population of this gorilla plummeted from around 17,000 in 1994 to about 3,800 in 2016, largely due to poaching for bushmeat.

Gorillas are strictly vegetarian. They feed mostly on bamboo shoots but also eat berries, nettles, and wild celery. They feed in the early morning and late afternoon, and they can sleep as much as 12 hours throughout the evening. The gorillas seen in zoos are almost all the smaller, lowland gorillas, which also live in the DRC.

It is estimated that the DRC has lost 70 percent of the eastern lowland gorilla and some 75 percent of the bonobo in the last decade. Habitat loss and hunting are the greatest threats, though these magnificent primates also live under the sword of the Ebola virus. Human contact has brought an extra threat to the already endangered existence of these great apes: They are catching human diseases such as measles. In addition, when thousands of refugees fled through the Virunga Reserve into Zaire in 1994, the great apes were forced into colder, higher areas, where they now run the risk of catching pneumonia. Some have already died in game traps set to catch other animals for food. The remaining gorillas are now trapped inside a shrinking forest that remains a war zone.

in Asia. Poaching is placing the African forest elephant in serious jeopardy. As the road infrastructure for logging explodes across the Congo Basin, the area of remote wilderness is decreasing rapidly, allowing poachers access to the last herds in the depths of the forest. In the country's largest forested national park, Salonga National Park in the remote heart of the DRC, only 1,700 elephants were counted in 2013, and the number is probably much lower now.

An elephant calf nuzzles its mother in the Congo rainforest.

NATIONAL PARKS

Five of Congo's eleven national parks have been named as UNESCO World Heritage Sites. Although the parks were established to protect endangered animals, the parks themselves are endangered. Virunga National Park suffered extensive damage by armed bands of soldiers and refugees from neighboring camps, who harvested 36 million trees from the park and hunted gorillas and other animals. Garamba National Park, near Sudan, was raided by Sudanese soldiers hunteding endangered wildlife using automatic weapons. Okapi Wildlife Reserve, within the Ituri Forest and home to more species of primates than anywhere else in the world, has been ravaged by refugee migrations and marauding bands of militias, who looted and stole conservation equipment and killed park staff.

GARAMBA NATIONAL PARK Garamba National Park was home to the world's last known wild population of northern white rhinoceroses. Due to poaching of the rhinos within the park, in 1996 it was added to the list of World Heritage Sites in danger.

KAHUZI-BIÉGA NATIONAL PARK Kahuzi-Biéga National Park is in eastern DRC, near the western side of Lake Kivu and the Rwandan border. The park is one of the last refuges of the rare mountain gorilla and was where the renowned American primatologist Dian Fossey studied gorillas before relocating to Rwanda.

MAIKO NATIONAL PARK Maiko National Park lies in one of the most remote forest areas of the DRC. Three of the country's spectacular endemic animals live here: the eastern lowland gorilla, the okapi, and the Congo peacock.

OKAPI WILDLIFE RESERVE The Okapi Wildlife Reserve is a World Heritage Site in the Ituri Forest in the northeast of the DRC, near the borders with Sudan and Uganda. As implied by the name, the reserve is home to many okapis. It is home to many other interesting or endangered animals as well, including the forest elephant and at least thirteen species of primates. Nomadic Mbuti pygmies and indigenous Bantu farmers also live within the reserve.

A guide and a park ranger talk with tourists in Virunga National Park.

THE DEMISE OF THE NORTHERN WHITE RHINO

The DRC's Garamba National Park, on the border with Sudan, was—until recently—home to the world's only surviving wild population of northern white rhinoceros

(Ceratotherium simum cottoni). The animals once lived in abundance throughout northeastern DRC, the Central African Republic, and parts of Chad, Sudan, and Uganda. They are one of two subspecies of white rhinoceros, the other being the southern white rhinoceros.

At one time, visitors could view the rhinos while riding on elephants. As late as 1960, there were still around 2,360 northern white rhinos remaining. But as with the elephant's tusk, the rhino is prized for its horn by people (primarily in Asia) who believe it has medicinal or magical powers. The price of rhino horn on the black market was and still is so high that some desperately poor African people are willing to risk their lives to obtain it. These poachers have decimated the population of northern white rhinos to extinction. The violence of past civil wars in the region also hurt the wildlife population.

The southern white rhinos is doing somewhat better. Conservation efforts to relocate, or translocate as the practice is called, enough of those animals to safer environments brought the number of that species from less than one hundred to around twenty thousand in the wild today. Translocating a three- or four-ton beast is no easy matter.

In 1984, when some fifteen of the animals lived in Garamba, conservationists rallied to try to save the species. Their efforts brought the numbers up to about thirty individuals by 2003. However, poaching increased again and international agencies worked out an emergency plan to translocate the animals. The DRC government refused. However, that same government proved unable to protect the animals, or even the park rangers hired to protect them. The Garamba park became essentially unmanageable and the rhinos suffered as a result. By 2014, there were none left alive in the park.

As of 2018, there are only three of the animals left on earth—one male and two females—all in well-protected conservancy in Kenya. Although scientists have been trying to produce offspring, the remaining male is old and the efforts have not worked.

SALONGA NATIONAL PARK Salonga National Park is located in the Congo River Basin. It is Africa's largest tropical rain-forest reserve. Animals in the park include bonobos, Salonga and Tshuapa red colobus monkeys, Congo peacocks, forest elephants, and African slender-snouted crocodiles. It gained the status of a UNESCO World Heritage Site in 1984.

UPEMBA NATIONAL PARK Upemba National Park is a large park in Katanga Province. Located in a lush area dotted by lakes, including Lake Upemba, and bordered by the Lualaba River, it dominates the Kibara Plateau. Upemba National Park is home to some 1,800 species of plants and animals. There are also a handful of villages in the park. In recent years the park has come under considerable attack from poachers and local militias.

LOGGING

A 2014 Chatham House report found that nearly 90 percent of logging in the DRC is illegal or unmanaged. The actual wood harvest is estimated to be about eight times larger than official government numbers. Despite the country's 2002 Forest Code moratorium on new logging, enforcement of the law has been weak to say the least. Like many other sectors of the Congo government, the Forestry Department is underfunded, badly managed, susceptible to corruption, and almost completely ineffective.

Even legal logging activities pose a threat to the forests, as the incursion of logging roads open up previously impenetrable jungle to other human activities, such as poaching. Illegal and unmanaged logging harms local communities, as conflict between illegal loggers and forest communities often results in violence and sometimes murder. Logging also threatens biodiversity and worsens climate change. It also results in lost revenue for poorer governments such as Congo's. A government too weak to manage its forests is also too weak to collect the proper fees from loggers, which is exactly what's occurring. Therefore, loggers may be essentially stealing the country's natural resources.

Virunga, on the Rwanda and Uganda borders, is one of the oldest and most spectacular national parks in Africa. Due to both Congolese civil wars and poaching, however, there has been a 98 percent plunge in the hippo population, and other species are also at risk. Nevertheless, dedicated park workers are devoted to the park's protection. Although mountain gorillas are now extremely rare, successful conservation work has secured the remaining populations. The terrain is a mixture of grassy plains and marshy river mouths at the lower levels and equatorial mountain forests and snowfields in the higher areas.

Many tourists used to combine viewing the natural life of Virunga with a visit to the neighboring volcanic park, with its active volcanoes Nyiragongo (which last erupted in 2010) and Nyamulagira (which last erupted in 2011).

Virunga National Park lies completely within the borders of the DRC. The famous gorilla sanctuary area, a UNESCO World Heritage Site, is adjacent on the east and spans the borders of the DRC, Uganda, and Rwanda. It was from this sanctuary that the American primatologist Dian Fossey led a campaign to save mountain gorillas from extinction—and it was here, on December 26, 1985, that she was found hacked to death by still-unknown assailants.

The Senkwekwe Center at the park headquarters in Rumangabo, is the only facility in the world that cares for mountain gorilla orphans. Young gorillas are occasionally found in the wild that have been traumatized by poachers and animal traffickers who killed the other members of the animal's family. They are nursed back to health and live out their lives at this center.

In 2015, BBC reported that the DRC wanted to redraw the boundaries of Virunga National Park to allow for oil exploration.

A young girl stands on a heavily littered riverbank in Kinshasa.

ONGOING DAMAGE TO THE ENVIRONMENT

Weak government enforcement affects a wide range of environmental problems. Indiscriminate dumping of raw sewage into the rivers has resulted in 70 percent of the rural population not having access to safe water, as well as outbreaks of diseases such as cholera. Pollution from oil rigs has contaminated the DRC's fish populations, and crude oil from the rigs sticks to fishermen's nets. People fall ill after eating the infected fish, and officials at the Ministry of Environment have found that hydrocarbon pollution in the water around the refineries is more than seven times the normal level. The oil companies are a big source of employment and finance for the DRC, which is why many officials are reluctant to antagonize the oil corporations. The two Congo Wars also meant that issues on pollution reduction or control had to take a backseat while politicians struggled for power. To add to the DRC's environmental woes, air pollution is high due to vehicle emissions.

INTERNET LINKS

http://www.bbc.com/news/world-africa-31876577
This interesting story highlights the conflict between park conservation and economic potential.

https://blog.nationalgeographic.org/2016/09/04/grauers-gorilla-at-extremely-high-risk-of-extinction-in-the-wild
Maps and large photos accompany this article about endangered gorillas in the DRC.

https://news.mongabay.com/2014/04/nearly-90-percent-of-logging-in-the-drc-is-illegal
This article focuses on logging in the Congo forests.

https://www.savetherhino.org
This conservation site has articles and statistics about the demise of the white rhino in DRC.

https://www.theguardian.com/environment/2010/sep/07/congo-chimpanzees-bushmeat
This is a shocking article on the hunting of chimpanzees for the bushmeat trade.

http://whc.unesco.org/en/statesparties/cd
This is the World Heritage directory for sites in the DRC.

https://virunga.org
This official site of Virunga National Park is available in English.

CONGOLESE

A woman in Lukonga balances a market basket on her head, as is the custom.

6

THE DEMOCRATIC REPUBLIC OF THE Congo is a very diverse country, made up of hundreds of ethnic groups of various origins. Racially, however, the people are almost entirely black Africans with deep ancestral roots.

The number of people who live in this huge nation, with its vast jungles, has never been established with complete accuracy. Informed estimates in 2017 gave the DRC a population of around 83 million people. The Population Reference Bureau in Washington, DC, has estimated that by the year 2050, the DRC will be the second most populous nation in Africa, with 189.3 million people, after Nigeria (282.2 million people). Almost half (42 percent) of the population is under the age of fifteen.

THE ETHNIC GROUPS

The Congolese do not belong to clear ethnic groups. There are more than 250 tribal groups, and not one accounts for more than 4 percent of the total population. More than two-thirds of the tribes are Bantu. Bantu is used as a general label for more than four hundred ethnic groups in sub-Saharan Africa. These peoples share a common language family subgroup, the Bantu languages. The population also includes people of Sudanese and Nilotic (early Egyptian) origin and pygmies. A very small number of Europeans, mostly of Belgian origin, remain. And increasingly, hundreds of thousands of refugees from Rwanda, Burundi, and Angola add to the diversity.

According to the US census there are about twenty thousand DRC-born people living in the United States. However, many US citizens can no doubt trace their genetic ancestry to Congolese ethnic groups, as a large percentage of the enslaved people forced to migrate to North America several centuries ago came from Western and West-Central Africa.

Village children wave goodbye to UNICEF volunteers who provided tetanus inoculations.

THE LUBA This group is indigenous to the southeast-central part of the country but have spread widely. They live mostly in the Kasai, Maniema, and Katanga provinces region, north of Lubumbashi, and many work in the copper mines. Their dialect, Tshiluba, is widely spoken in the southeast, though many speak Kiswahili, or Swahili, as well. The Baluba, a subgroup, have a reputation for artistry, and Luba masks are among the most famous of Congolese/Zairean craftwork. Laurent Kabila, the late president, belonged to the Luba group.

THE MONGO This broad term refers to a number of ethnic groups living in the central part of the country, south of the Congo River. These groups speak dialects of a common language, Mongo or Nkundo. Their ancient, traditional religion includes a strong emphasis on ancestor worship. The people also believe in nature spirits, fertility rites, and magic, sorcery, and witchcraft, though today these are likely to be mixed with Christianity. Some Mongo tribes still practice polygamy, though missionaries have tried to end it. Traditionally, Mongo art was expressed orally, with a complex system of songs and talking-drum literature. The Mongo people cultivate cassava, yam, and plantains and also hunt and gather foods in the forests.

THE KUBA The Kuba kingdom was located in the southeastern region of the DRC. It reached its height three hundred years ago when its ninety-third king, Shamba Bolongongo, became a cultural hero. He is said to have introduced cassava, palm oil, tobacco, raffia, and embroidery to the area.

THE KONGO These people live in the western part of the country. The kingdom of Kongo was once the most powerful in Central Africa, extending into the lower reaches of the Congo and south into what is now Angola. Their rulers held the title *mani* (MAH-nee) and controlled their currency by using as money special shells found only in the waters fished by their ruling family.

With their kingdom located on the western coast of Africa, these relatively accessible people became frequent targets of European slave traders. Some 5.69 million Kongo people were captured and sent abroad as slaves—more than from any other single ethnic group.

Their dialect, Kikongo, is widely spoken in the country and is especially common in Kinshasa. Many Kongo people also speak French or Lingala.

THE AZANDE These people were late arrivals in the Congo region, invading from the northeast in the nineteenth century. They live primarily in three African countries: the DRC, South Sudan, and the Central African Republic. They are a Sudanese people and have their own religion based on Mani, the god of the rainbow. However, most have been converted to Christiantiy.

THE ALUR are a Nilotic race who live on the shore of Lake Mobutu, in the northeastern part of the country, where they are farmer-herders. Their culture is dominated by traditional kings and by priests who claim to possess the art of rainmaking.

THE MANGBETU live near the Bima River in the northeastern forests. Their area was prime hunting ground for Arab traders, who took many women and children hostage in exchange for ivory. Mangbetu mothers once practiced a custom called *Lipombo*, or head binding, in which they wound strips of cloth tightly around the heads of their newborn daughters so that their skulls became elongated. The Mangbetu were also known historically as a cannibalistic people.

THE LUNDA were once a proud Congolese empire led by a legendary king, Mwata Yamvo. The northern descendants of the Lunda still live in Katanga Province, but many have moved to Angola and Zambia and now speak a different language. Some still press for Katanga to break away as a separate country, hoping to revive the Lunda empire.

THE CHOKWE were originally a seminomadic Bantu-speaking people near the upper Kwango and Kasai rivers. Many became slavers for the Portuguese and so helped to destroy many neighboring kingdoms, including that of the Lunda. Known for their skill in carving sculptures of human and animal forms, the million and more Chokwe are now spread over a wide area that includes the southern DRC as well as adjacent parts of Angola and Zambia.

CHARACTERISTICS

The Congolese, like other Africans, know the importance of survival. To survive, one must have patience. To avoid stress, simply move with the pace of the system. People wait patiently in line to see the doctor or apply for a permit. They do not get frustrated if machines do not work or if goods are not available in the shops. So long as one has something to eat and wear, a modest shelter to call home, and the surrounding love of family, the world has treated one well. The Kiswahili speakers would say *"Shauriya Mungu"* (SHOW-reeyoh MUN-goo)—"It is God's will."

Yet all this patience typically vanishes when a Congolese is put behind the wheel of a car. He becomes a totally different personality and sees the car as a challenge to his manhood. The route from Kinshasa Airport to the city is probably the most used stretch of road in the country and a common place for car accidents.

The African tribal system stipulates that a man should look after his family first, then his clan, and finally his tribe. The idea of belonging to a nation is

PYGMIES

Pygmy people are members of certain ethnic groups characterized by their unusually short height. There are at least twelve different pygmy groups living in different parts of the DRC and neighboring African nations, about 250,000 to 600,000 people altogether.

A typical adult is little more than 4 feet (1.2 m) tall. He or she has brown skin, brown eyes, a snub nose, and thin lips. The older men may have a sparse, tufted beard. These small hunters of the northern rain forests were probably the earliest inhabitants of the Congo Basin. Nomadic, they move around in small groups, rarely settling anywhere for long. They live by hunting and fishing, working in groups, often using dogs. Both men and women gather food from the forests they know so well, collecting honey, nuts, and roots. Women tend their settlements and sometimes grow peanuts. The pygmies are pacifists by nature and hardly quarrel within their group. They are also very shy, and if surprised by the approach of strangers (which happens seldom, as they are acutely aware of all who live around them), they will drop everything and rush off into the forest.

They value children as their most precious possessions, as they must, for infant mortality is high. If parents die, children are passed on to another family group. In many groups there is no defined leader. All adults are called "mother" and "father" by all the children, and decisions are made by general agreement. Each group lives in communal style, with most possessions (apart from weapons) owned by all. They value life highly and will burst into spontaneous dancing and drumming, usually at night, around a fire.

Pygmies live mainly in the dense tangle of trees and undergrowth of the Ituri Forest region. They avoid forest clearings, which are fiercely hot. Those near the Epulu River and Mount Hoyo are becoming used to contact with Europeans. They will sit by the road, waiting to be photographed or just talked to, and will then demand a tip. Pygmies who interact with their fellow Congolese complain of discrimination and abuse. Such abuse was also seen in the colonial era when Belgian authorities sent pygmy children to zoos around the world, like animals, to be put on exhibit.

During the Congo conflict, particularly in 2002 and 2003, pygmies in the northeastern province of Ituri were hunted down, enslaved, and sometimes eaten as game animals. Government forces and rebel and militia groups, who regarded the pygmies as "subhuman," also believed that their flesh conferred magical powers.

not an important concept. What matters more is power, which should be held by one individual and not be weakened by being shared.

THE EXTENDED FAMILY From his earliest days, a Congolese baby is strapped to his or her mother's back and goes everywhere she goes, such as the fields to work or other places to collect wood or fetch water for home. By the time the next baby arrives, the growing child has absorbed a strong physical presence of love and care. So the child grows up obedient to the parents and with the awareness that there is nothing more important than the family. Although a young child is often left on his or her own, there are always brothers, sisters, or a grandparent around. The same extended family system is found in the shantytowns located around the big cities, but it tends to fade away with the nuclear family groups in towns.

REFUGEES

The DRC, which does not produce enough food to feed its own people, is host to hundreds of thousands of refugees and asylum seekers from neighboring countries—mostly from Rwanda, Central African Republic, South Sudan, and Burundi—and some 4.1 million internally displaced persons (IDP). In addition, armed conflicts and inter-ethnic fighting has driven thousands of Congolese to become refugees in neighboring countries such as Zambia. In 2017 alone, about 5,800 Congolese crossed the border into Zambia.

Counting the numbers of refugees both entering and leaving the country is difficult. In 2017, UNHCR, the UN Refugee Agency, reported 508,300 Congolese refugees residing in neighboring countries, in flight from the fighting in the eastern provinces. Likewise, the report stated that 537,087 refugees from other nations were in the DRC—and those are merely the ones who have officially registered with the authorities.

DRESS

A length of cloth, tied under the arms for a woman or around the waist for a man, is the simplest and cheapest form of clothing in Africa. The better-off may add a skirt, a pair of trousers, or a T-shirt, but in this hot land, no one needs a lot of clothing. Most families strive to have one good set of clothes for church or festive days.

The introduction of comparatively cheap clothing in the cities and markets has led to most urban folk dressing in conventional Western style. The men wear open-neck shirts with jeans or dark trousers and sneakers or brown or black leather shoes. Older men wear a hat. Most women wear a headscarf. Short skirts or tight pants for women are frowned on as being suggestive, particularly in the countryside.

INTERNET LINKS

https://www.catholicnewsagency.com/news/the-devastating-but -little-noticed-drc-refugee-crisis-78599
This article reports the rapid increase of refugees fleeing the DRC.

https://www.cnn.com/2012/11/09/world/africa/congo-sapeur -fashion/index.html
The Congolese Sapeur fashion cult of elegant dress is explored in this article

http://ngm.nationalgeographic.com/ngm/0509/feature5
"Who Rules the Forest?" is an article about the Mbuti Pygmies of Congo's Ituri Forest.

https://www.voanews.com/a/pygmies-of-central-africa-driven -from-ancestral-jungles--119688109/159756.html
This is another eye-opening article about the plight of the pygmy people in DRC.

http://worldpopulationreview.com/countries/dr-congo-population
This site keeps track of up-to-date population statistics with projections for the future.

LIFESTYLE

Traditional thatched roof houses make up a village in the North Kivu mountains.

7

WHAT IS THE LIFESTYLE OF A people in an impoverished, war-torn country? Life in the DRC isn't easy, to be sure, but except in areas of active fighting, daily life does go on. People still form families and friendships, raise children, work, eat what they can, and simply try to get by. Misery is certainly a fact of life in this dreadfully troubled nation, but so is singing, dancing, laughing, and loving.

POVERTY AND STARVATION

The first and constant problem is a lack of money and food. Farmers grow what they can to feed their families, but there is rarely any surplus to provide enough income for investment in more seed, better tools, or more land. With no social security system and little employment, many people turn to robbery, corruption, or begging. Young men with few prospects hitch a ride on an overland truck or a river steamer to go to a city, where they become just one more unemployed worker. Too ashamed to return home, they may turn to crime.

Many of the public schools in the Congo are in deplorable condition. In a rural school, children may sit on a bare earthen floor in a roofed shelter without windows. They are taught orally, since there are no books. If the school has a blackboard, it has to be taken down each afternoon to prevent it from being stolen.

A man feeds his goats while traveling on a barge on the Congo River.

GETTING AROUND

"The first problem is the roads," said a visitor. "There aren't any." During the rainy season, the tracks through forests or across wooded plains are so swampy or rocky that trucks have to be dug out of potholes as big as swimming pools.

The highways of the country are the waterways. Large riverboats once churned their way between Kinshasa and Kisangani, but today those old steamers sit as rusted out hulks. The main mode of travel is on barges pushed by tugs. Their timetable is erratic, as they tend to wait until they have gathered enough cargo and passengers to make the trip worthwhile. In addition to people, they carry battered trucks, rusty bicycles, crates of chickens, and tethered animals. The smell of rotting fish pervades everything.

On river crossings, the use of ferries is supposed to be free, but the fare is usually enough diesel for them to operate. Dugout canoes known as pirogues are used by fishermen as the waterborne equivalent of bicycles.

TRAVEL ON THE CONGO RIVER

Barges transport people and goods up and the down the rivers. Each has a big tugboat with four or five rusty barges attached. This "floating city" departs from one terminus fully booked and loaded, then accumulates as much as double the load along the way until it arrives with as many as three thousand people aboard. Almost as many travel on the roofs of the barges as inside.

For those who live by the river, the river barges offer an opportunity for trade. All along the route, vendors paddle wooden pirogues out from the forested shore and tie up to the side of the riverboat. Their owners haul their wares on board and sell them. Goods for sale include cassava and monkeys, hand-woven mats and edible maggots, dried catfish and live snapping turtles. In fact, the decks become a menagerie of Congolese wildlife. Ducks, geese, chickens, goats, and pigs are normal, and they may be joined by crocodiles, parrots, anteaters, bushbucks, or otters. Some animals die on the way and are cut up and added to the stock in the freezer or tipped overboard. Small-time traders have permanently booked cabins that become shops selling clothing, soap, cosmetics, plastic buckets, and medicines. As the pirogues sellers paddle home, more arrive. Business continues all day and night.

In the cities, the well-known "bush taxi" may be an old Peugeot 504, a well-dented minibus, or a pickup truck with wooden seats. It is always crammed to capacity, and the passengers will howl with mirth every time the vehicle jolts into yet another pothole and yet another head hits the roof. The railway system, built by the Belgians, used to be quite good. There is no longer a first-class service (despite the printed tickets), since there is likely to be no water or lighting available, and quite probably no windows or doors. Traveling from one end of the DRC to the other can take a month, unless the journey is by plane.

CITY LIFE

The contrast between urban and rural life is distinctly marked. Kinshasa, with approximately 11 million people, boasts skyscrapers such as the Intercontinental Hotel with its luxurious shops and suites, while in the rain forests pygmies live as primitive hunter-gatherers did thousands of years ago. In some parts of the city, piles of refuse lay stinking in the streets, litter blows around, few water taps or telephones work, and the buildings are grimy and damp with mold. "River people" live in shanties built of rubbish on islands and under bridges.

Yet even in the squalor and poverty, the residents continue to live and laugh. The pulse of Kinshasa is still in the vibrant African quarter with its backyard bars, street corner catering, and live music for which the country is internationally renowned. Other cities—Lubumbashi, Kisangani, Mbuji-Mayi—are nowhere near as large as Kinshasa. Their hotels are less luxurious, and their shantytowns are less populated. But they are all plagued with the same two problems: the absence of any state money to make repairs or pay officials and a steady influx of rural migrants hoping to find food, shelter, and work in town.

COUNTRY LIFE

To outsiders, the rural Congolese may appear to own nothing, but this does not prevent them from offering fruit, water, or shade to welcome a visitor. Their sense of hospitality may result in a feast of roasted groundnuts, grilled corn, or elephant meat.

Most dwellings are of mud bricks or wood with woven walls. A central meetinghouse or shelter called the *da* doubles as accommodation for guests. It may contain a bamboo bed, or *kiri-pa* (KEE-ree-PAH), for visitors to lie on. Aromas in the air might include those of drying cassava, which smells a bit like yeasty bread, or meat being roasted if a hunter has returned with a kill.

The women go to the fields each day to gather what is required and restock by continual planting. They will return with cassava, which is peeled and soaked, then dried and crushed before being pounded in a wooden mortar for cooking. This is an ongoing process that may take a week or more.

Men go hunting, armed perhaps with a shotgun or with homemade guns. Their sons practice earnestly with a bow and arrow or with catapults. Because there are no telephones, people shout the news down the village street.

EDUCATION

The first schools in the DRC were started by missionaries, and these Catholic and Protestant schools remain vital. It is a wonder, of course, that education continues at all in a country torn by war and in which teachers have remained unpaid for long periods.

Indeed, during the civil wars of the late 1990s—early 2000s, more than 5.2 million children in the country did not receive any schooling at all. In war-torn eastern provinces, where some 2 million people have had to flee their homes, many children are still growing up without any formal education. Even where schools are available, many parents have been afraid to send their children, for fear of having them kidnapped by rebel armies, which are well known for using child soldiers. Although there has been some progress in improving the country's education system and attendance statistics, the DRC is still one of the countries with the largest number of out-of-school children.

A teacher instructs students at a community center for AIDS orphans, victims, and others displaced by armed conflict in Goma.

However, the Congolese respect education and want their children to have its advantages. Primary education, from ages six to twelve, is neither compulsory nor free nor universal. Statistics are sketchy, but UNICEF reports that between 2008 and 2012, some 77.5 percent of boys and 72.1 percent of girls attended primary school. Of those, just over half stayed in school through fifth grade. Secondary school participation was much lower, with 35.1 percent of boys and 28.3 percent of girls attending. Secondary schools include schools of general education, teacher-training colleges, and technical schools. There are university campuses in Kinshasa, Kisangani, Lubumbashi, and Goma.

However, not all teachers are themselves sufficiently educated. Almost 74 percent of primary teachers are qualified, but only 33 percent of secondary level teachers. Either way, teacher salaries are extremely low—about $35–$40 a month, or less—and parents are often asked to help scrape those salaries together when the state is not forthcoming with the funds. In primary school, a teacher has an average of thirty-seven students, but in marginalized or rural areas, there can be more than one hundred pupils per class.

Though statistics report increasing numbers of children going to school, the quality of the education they receive is often quite low. Nevertheless, literacy rates are rising. After a decline in literacy following the civil war years 1998–2003, the percentage of people over age fifteen who can read and write (at a very basic level) in French, Lingala, Kingwana, or Tshiluba has improved greatly. In 2016, about 77 percent of the population was deemed literate—88.5 percent of the men and 66.5 percent of the women.

HEALTH

The medical facilities in the country are appalling. Equipment does not work, perhaps because people have stolen pieces of it, and often there is no electricity or water. Patients lie in hospital corridors because the wards are full, and frequently they must share a bed. At Kinshasa General Hospital, the sick must supply their own drugs, bedding, food, and syringes. Animals wander in, and the state of cleanliness is highly suspect. Many health clinics have shut down because the medicines intended for their use have been intercepted and sold on the black market.

A lack of sustaining food and proper health care is particularly hard on children. The mortality rate of children under five years old has fallen to almost half what it was in 1990. However, with increasing population growth, the number of children who die before their fifth birthday has increased—from 280,000 in 1990 to 304,000 in 2016. The first month of life is the most vulnerable, with the neonatal mortality rate having risen since 1990, from 22 percent to 30 percent in 2016. Nearly one-quarter of all children are underweight. Hundreds of children die every day, many due to malaria. The disease kills about 300,000 Congolese children under five every year. The moist, humid conditions of the rain forests are an ideal breeding ground for the aedes mosquito, which spreads dengue fever, yellow fever, and other diseases.

THE ROLE OF WOMEN

The DRC is sometimes called "the world's worst place to be a woman." It is also commonly called "the rape capital of the world," which reinforces the notion that it's a very, very bad place to be female.

It is a patriarchal society to be sure. Men, especially the elders of the community, are viewed as the most important members. Women are expected to work for their men, and they accept this role in society. It is not unusual to see an old woman staggering along a village street with a huge load of food on her head while her husband lolls back in the doorway with an empty bottle of alcohol in his hand. Wife beating is not uncommon.

Yet women are the backbone of every rural community. They plant and tend crops and harvest the food. They run the markets, which are the prime economic activity of the village.

A law imposed in 1987 and known as Mobutu's Family Code gives a husband the right to claim all of his wife's property, even if they are not living together. Polygamy was legalized, and husbands were relieved of any responsibility for the maintenance of their women and children. As a rule wives do not inherit from their husband, and they can be divorced without settlement. Indeed

Known in the Congo by its French acronym, SIDA, AIDS (acquired immune deficiency syndrome) has devastated the population of sub-Saharan Africa. Caused by a virus called HIV (human immunodeficiency virus), which is transferrable from one person to another through exposure to bodily fluids, AIDS is the final, deadly stage of HIV infection. HIV attacks a person's immune system, making it too weak to fight off other infections or cancers. Although there is no cure, there are now medicines that help keep the HIV virus in check, preventing the infection from progressing to AIDS.

Medical researchers believe HIV/AIDS began sometime in the twentieth century in western equatorial Africa, not far from the Congo. The virus probably mutated from a close relative found in chimpanzees, apes, and monkeys and was passed to humans through contact with the flesh of infected chimps. Although viral transmission spread rapidly through sub-Saharan Africa, it wasn't until the 1980s, when it spread to the United States, that it was identified and given a name.

The pandemic took millions of lives in sub-Saharan Africa, greatly lowering the life expectancy rates in the hardest-hit areas. The disease also ravaged economies as it primarily killed off adults between the ages of twenty and forty-nine, at the height of their working lives. In the wake of those deaths, the pandemic left a generation of AIDS orphans—by 2001, some 11 million children in sub-Saharan Africa had been orphaned

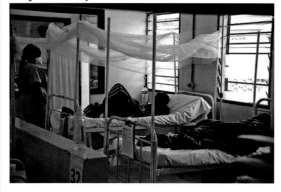

HIV patients are treated at a center run by Médecins San Frontières (Doctors Without Borders) in Lingala.

after both parents died of AIDS.

The DRC was and continues to be hard hit by AIDS, though things are slowly improving. The number of new incidents of HIV infection has fallen considerably since its height in the late 1990s. In 2012, about 480,000 people, or 1.1 percent of the DRC population, were living with HIV infection; by 2016, that number was 370,000, or 0.7 percent. Nineteen thousand Congolese people died of AIDS that year alone. At least 390,000 Congolese children are

AIDS orphans. HIV-infected mothers can inadvertently pass the virus to their unborn babies, and so there are at least 48,000 children in the DRC who are themselves infected with HIV.

in some areas a widow is expected to pay off her dead husband's debts; this "purifies" her from the suspicion of having killed her husband. Wives today are hoping that the new government will annul this family code.

The wars and conflicts have made the lives of women more perilous. Violence against women is thought by large sectors of society as normal. The number of women is decreasing rapidly in the Congo. Women are raped and kept as slaves for men, and when they are finally released, they sometimes kill themselves or check into a hospital, where they die anyway because the brutal assaulters have ruined their bodies internally.

During the past few years Congolese women have increasingly taken on the role of head of household because men have been unable to support their families or have died.

INTERNET LINKS

https://reliefweb.int/report/democratic-republic-congo/food -insecurity-soars-conflict-ridden-democratic-republic-congo
This humanitarian site reports on food insecurity in the DRC.

http://www.slate.com/articles/news_and_politics/roads/2015/09 /congo_by_barge_giant_overstuffed_river_barges_are_the_best_ way_to_get_from.html
This first-person narrative paints a colorful picture of travel on a Congo River barge.

http://time.com/platon-congo-denis-mukwege
This photo essay deals with the extremely difficult subject of sexual violence against women as a strategy of war, and the people in the Congo who are helping women to heal.

https://www.unicef.org/infobycountry/drcongo_statistics.html
UNICEF provides statistics on health, education, hunger, AIDS, and other relevant life factors in the DRC.

RELIGION

A girl sings at the Mulamo Baptist Church in Butembo, North Kivu.

8

THE CONGOLESE ARE VERY religious people. More than 70 percent of them attend religious services weekly; and of those, 90 percent follow some form of Christianity. Indeed, Christianity has deep roots in Africa. However, indigenous religions and beliefs have even deeper roots, and many people in the Congo worship in ways that combine the two.

CHRISTIANITY

Christianity was established in parts of Africa well before it reached Europe. Although Christianity first reached Egypt and Ethiopia, it was the Portuguese who brought it to the Kongo people in the area around the mouth of the Congo River. Soon after the explorers came the missionaries. Many thought Africans to be unenlightened and backward, and the Europeans regarded it as their duty to save the souls of such unfortunate people. To that supposedly noble end, they imposed the Christian faith and culture on the people, by force if necessary.

Today, most Congolese follow some form of Christianity—50 percent are Roman Catholics, and 20 percent are Protestants. No more than 10 percent of the population is Muslim; they live mainly in the northeast corner of the country among the Azande.

In December 2016, Congo's Catholic bishops brokered a peace deal between President Joseph Kabila's regime and the opposition. Among the demands were that the government free all political prisoners; end the harassment of opposition politicians; and Kabila leave office by December 19, 2017. When Kabila did not step down, Pope Francis put off a planned visit to the DRC, saying he wouldn't come until after the country holds elections.

Cardinal Laurent Monsengwo Pasinya *(center)*, the Archbishop of Kinshasa, leads a Catholic mass in September 2016 to mourn victims of recent political violence in the city.

The Roman Catholic and Protestant churches control a large proportion of the hospitals, dispensaries, and schools in the country that were built by mission stations and are still run largely by dedicated mission workers. Church workers have set up agricultural, stockbreeding, and housing projects for the Congolese. It is said that almost every president in Africa has been the product of a missionary education.

The African churches, however, have a definite African flavor. A church service may take place in a church or a chapel or under a canvas awning in the open air. There is much dancing and hand clapping, and the sermon is long because it is often delivered in French with an interpreter enthusiastically translating it into the local dialect. And many Congolese Christians also happily include indigenous tribal practices in their spiritual lives, finding that the different religions enrich each other.

SYNCRETIC CHRISTIAN-AFRICAN RELIGIONS

A number of syncretic, or hybrid, sects exist in the country, which merge Christianity with inidgenous beliefs and rituals.

JAMAA This faith was founded by a Franciscan missionary from Belgium, Father Placide Tempels (1906—1977), who preached a message of fraternity not unlike that of the early church in Jerusalem. In 1954 seven married Catholic couples in Ruwe, near Kolwezi in South Katanga, formed the Jamaa movement based on his teachings. *Jamaa* (ja-MAH) is the Kiswahili word for "family." The converts call each other *baba* and *mama*, Kiswahili for "father" and "mother." The Virgin Mary is often referred to by her Bantu name, Mama Maria. The Jamaa creed is embraced in three themes: life, fecundity, and vital union. Faith must be lived and discovered through sharing in the Christian community, and from this relationship come children: not newborn babies but newborn adults, all part of an ever-growing, spiritual family. Since all members join as married couples, women assume a much higher status than is usual in Congolese society.

Tempels argued against the accepted European view that African people and their cultures were inferior, primitive, and savage. He said that Christianity had to be presented within the context of a unified African culture. He published his thinking in a book titled *Bantu Philosophy*, which was met with considerable opposition, especially among the hierarchy of the Church. Though the charismatic Jamaa movement continued to grow, Tempels was forcibly retired to Belgium in 1962.

KIMBANGUIST CHURCH About 10 percent of the Congolese belong to the Kimganguist Church, the largest independent African church. Its full title is The Church of Jesus Christ on Earth Through the Prophet Simon Kimbangu. It was founded by Simon Kimbangu (1887—1951), who grew up in a Baptist Missionary Society mission in the Belgian Congo. He became famous as a preacher and healer among the Kongo people. The thousands who came to hear his preaching called him *Ngunza*, the Kikongo word for "prophet."

Belgian authorities became alarmed by the large crowds he attracted and the occasional disturbances they caused. Along with religious teachings, Kimbangu preached that black Congolese, not white Belgian colonizers, should rule the country. For that, he and his closest followers were arrested in September 1921. He spent the rest of his life in prison in what is now Lubumbashi and died there in October 1951.

Children play flutes at a Kimbanguist religious service in the city of Beni.

His youngest son, Joseph Diangienda, founded the Kimbanguist Church and it gained official recognition in 1959. It was the first African church to be admitted, in 1969, to the World Council of Churches. The church has spread widely in Central Africa. Followers believe "Papa" Simon Kimbangu was a special envoy of Jesus Christ. They also believe that a grandson who shares his name, and who was born in October 1951 as Kimbangu was dying, is the Holy Spirit. In fact, Simon Kimbangu Kiangani, who now leads the church, claims to be not only the Holy Spirit, but also the reincarnation of Papa Simon Kimbangu.

The church's creed rejects violence, polygamy, magic and witchcraft, alcohol, tobacco, and dancing. The worship is Baptist in form; communion was introduced in 1971. The Kimbanguist Church supports a large amount of social work in agriculture, healing, education, and youth work.

TRADITIONAL AFRICAN RELIGIONS

Indigenous beliefs vary, but in general, most acknowledge one god, the Creator. However, followers of traditional practices don't invest much spiritual energy in this god because the Creator is not involved much in human lives. Rather, people are more concerned with dead ancestors and nature spirits, which figure more directly on everyday life. Witches and sorcerers are thought to be people endowed with special powers who can direct misfortune or protection upon targeted individuals.

Nature spirits inhabit particular places, such as rivers, rocks, and trees, or in natural forces such as wind and lightning. In much of the northern DRC, for example, is the common practice to toss a small red item into a river before crossing it, to appease the river spirit. This ensures that an angry spirit won't stir up the waters and sink the boat.

Many believe humans must guard themselves against evil spirits. So amulets or fetishes are not considered magic; they are objects filled with power, put there by the blessing of a diviner or a holy man. Likewise, the charm seller in the marketplace offers wise advice on how to avoid danger. There is a special evil spirit, often called *li* (lee), who lives in the stomach of certain people and gives them an urge to wander around and create mischief. If such people can obtain a lock of hair, a fingernail clipping, or a piece of clothing from a person, then they may cast a spell that can lead to sickness or death. For this reason all cuttings on the floor of a barbershop are burned.

The Ngbandi tribal spirit is a snake, and the Ngbandi believe all twins are snakes. Therefore a twin dare not kill a snake, for that would be akin to killing himself. The Mbuti pygmies of the Ituri Forest perform a special dance before they go hunting to apologize to the animal spirit they are going to kill. Travelers throw a stone in every stream they cross to thank the river god for keeping the water flowing.

Many of the tribes along the Congo River believe in the mermaidlike water spirit Mama Wata, or Mami Wata ("Mother of Water"), who may bring wealth or death, and is also involved in healing rituals. Images of her are sold as good luck charms.

A man paints a mural of Mami Wata.

CHURCH AND STATE

Christian missionaries in the Congo region were not without controversy. For a while there was rivalry between Catholic and Protestant missionaries. There were claims that Protestants wanted to see the end of Belgian rule in the Congo, while the Catholic schools were careful to teach subservience and loyalty to Bula Matari—"Breaker of Rocks"—as the Zairean state was sometimes called. Today, foreign missionaries mostly work directly under the supervision of a Congolese-run church.

It is not uncommon for a dictator to portray himself as more divine than human. (See, for example, the deification of Kim Jong Un, the president of North Korea.) During Mobutu's reign, he encouraged Zairians to regard and adulate him as almost a god. The state-controlled media spoke of him as "the Guide, the Father of the Nation, the Chief, the Helmsman" and virtually as a messiah. "God has sent a great prophet, our prestigious Guide Mobutu" was the belief officially encouraged. Press releases about the president used capital letters when referring to "Him." They encouraged the population to replace crucifixes with a picture of Mobutu. His mother, Mama Yemo, was compared to the Virgin Mary. Millions across the country wore shirts printed with his picture.

However, those in missionary work represented a large proportion of the educated adults in the country. At the time of independence in 1960, some 15 percent of the non-African workforce was connected to the church. There were 7,500 missionaries in the Belgian Congo, of whom 6,000 were Catholic, many of them active in the health sector. The first native Congolese Catholic priest was ordained in 1917, the first Congolese bishop in 1956. In 1937 native priests numbered only 37; by 1960, there were nearly 400.

Church leaders in Africa have seldom hesitated to assume a role as guardians of the public conscience. Archbishop Desmond Tutu, for example, famously denounced apartheid in South Africa for many years. In the 1970s, in Mobutu's Zaire, Joseph Cardinal Malula (Joseph-Albert Malula, 1917–1989) did much to Africanize Catholic church rituals. The first native cardinal from Zaire, he introduced a totally African leadership in the Catholic Church—despite an ongoing feud with the president—following his vision of "a Congolese Church in a Congolese State."(In 2010, DRC President Joseph Kabila proclaimed Cardinal Malula "a national hero.")

President Mobutu, although a staunch Catholic, did all he could to reduce the power of the church. As part of his Africanization program, he decreed that everyone born after February 16, 1972, should be given names commemorating their ancestors, not Christian saints. In 1972 all religious radio and television programs were banned, and religious youth groups were forbidden in favor of "youth party branches.""It is the MPR [Popular Movement of the Revolution, the ruling party] and not the church that will lead the way," said Mobutu.

Today the government generally respects freedom of religion in practice, provided that worshipers neither disturb public order nor contradict commonly held morals.

INTERNET LINKS

https://africa.si.edu/exhibits/mamiwata/intro.html
The African water spirit Mami Wata is the subject of an art exhibit and essay on this Smithsonian site.

https://dacb.org/stories/democratic-republic-of-congo /malula3-joseph
An overview of the life and contributions of Joseph Malulu is presented on this Dictionary of African Christian Biography site.

https://www.nationalgeographic.com/photography/proof/2017/05 /africa-congo-uncanny-faith
This article and accompanying photographs take a peek into traditional faith practices in Congolese churches.

http://www.newsweek.com/can-catholic-church-save -congo-526886
This article examines the role the Catholic Church plays in the political realm of Congo.

https://www.oikoumene.org/en/member-churches/church-of-jesus -christ-on-earth-by-his-special-envoy-simon-kimbangu
This is the World Council of Churches page about the Kimbangu religion.

LANGUAGE

A newspaper stand displays French-language publications.

9

THE CONTINENT OF AFRICA HAS more than 1,700 distinct languages— almost one-third of all the languages in the world. In the DRC, there are more than two hundred languages and dialects spoken. Nearly all are Bantu languages, part of what linguists call the Niger-Congo linguistic family. Swahili, for instance, is a Bantu language of the Niger-Congo subcontinent, although it has strong Arabic influences.

THE MAIN LANGUAGES

There is no national Congolese language in the way that Spain has Spanish and Portugal has Portuguese. The official language is French, but it is somewhat despised as a colonial language forced on the country by European conquerors. French is the language of businesses, administrations, schools, newspapers and televisions, but even today there are many Congolese who do not speak French. Those that do, speak it almost universally as a second language. Therefore, French functions as a *lingua franca*, a common means of communication used by people who speak different languages. French is widely spoken in Kinshasa, the capital, and is also the predominant written language.

The Democratic Republic of the Congo is the world's most populous Francophone country. It's a Francophone country because its official language is French. And it is the world's most populous such country. However, in terms of actual speakers of French, there are more in France than in the DRC. Only about 40 percent of the Congolese people speak French, and almost all of them speak it as a second language.

Amid all of the regional and local languages of the DRC, four indigenous tongues have the status of national languages: Lingala, Kikongo, Swahili, and Tshiluba. In Kinshasa and along the Congo River as far as Kisangani, Lingala is spoken. Kikongo is spoken in the southwest between Kinshasa and the Atlantic, a reminder of the Kongo kingdom that once existed there. In East and West Kasai in the southern center of the country, Tshiluba is the most common tongue. The influence of the slavers from the Zanzibar Coast is clear in Kivu and the eastern border region, as well as around Lubumbashi, where Swahili is widely used as a first or second language. Around Goma, people speak Nandé.

Most Congolese languages and dialects derive from a Bantu base and are therefore tonal languages. This means that each word form can be pronounced in four or five tones to give different shades of meaning. The pitch of the voice determines the exact meaning of a word or phrase.

Bantu languages use prefixes for shades of meaning in the way that most European languages use suffixes. So, in the language of the Kongo, the people are Bakongo and the language is Kikongo—with *Ba* being a plural prefix and *Ki* indicating a language, as is also seen in the word *Kiswahili*, meaning "Swahili language." Kikongo is spoken by about 4.2 million people.

LINGALA This language grew out of the Bobangi language, which was spoken by the Bangala people. Historically, it was used as a trade language along the Congo River, and when the Europeans arrived in the late nineteenth century, it became the lingua franca in the northwestern part of the country, used by administrators and missionaries. As a trade language, it naturally picked up vocabulary from many sources, eventually emerging as a sort of combination language. Until about 1900, there was no written form, and missionaries were the first to devise one, a task which also required an attempt at standardizing the language. Around that time, the language took on the name Lingala. Today there are various ways to write it, all using the Latin alphabet, and there is no standardized spelling. Lingala is still mainly a spoken language, with over 10 million speakers, and it is the official language of the Congolese Army. Literacy in Lingala is low among Lingala speakers.

SWAHILI Also called Kiswahili, this tongue arrived in the Congo region as the language of the slave-trading caravans from Zanzibar, where it had developed as a mixture of African and Arab vocabularies. The Arabic word *sawahili* means "of the coast," and there is a group of Swahili people on the east coast of Tanzania. Swahili is now far more than a tribal language. It is rapidly becoming one of the international languages of Africa, spoken by almost 5 million people as their native tongue, and another 135 million as a second language.

Swahili is said to be the easiest African language for English speakers to learn. One reason is that it's one of the few sub-Saharan languages that's not tonal, just as English is not tonal. In written form, Swahili sounds just the way it reads.

AFRICANIZATION

In an attempt to rid his country of colonial influence, Mobutu aimed to "Africanize" all names under the cry of *authenticité* (OR-then-TISS-ee-tay), or "authenticity." So the capital city of Léopoldville became Kinshasa, Elisabethville became Lubumbashi, and Stanleyville was transformed into Kisangani. The province of Katanga was changed to Shaba, the Kiswahili word for "copper."

After Mobutu met with Ugandan president Idi Amin Dada, Lakes Albert and Edward were renamed Lake Mobutu Sese Seko and Lake Idi Amin Dada. Mobutu ordered his people to replace their Christian names with African ones; he himself changed his name from Joseph Désiré Mobutu to Mobutu Sese Seko. His full "praise name" was announced as Mobutu Sese Seko Kuku Ngbenduwaza Banga. Mobutu wore his famous leopard skin cap as a visual indication of his Africanness.

ZAIRE OR CONGO? Mobutu renamed the country and its great river Zaïre, with an umlaut over the i in the French manner, because he thought that it was a more African name than Congo. In fact it is a Portuguese mispronunciation of the ancient Kikongo word *nzere* or *nzadi*, meaning "the river that swallows

The French-speaking people of sub-Saharan Africa make up one third of the world's French speakers. When North African speakers are included, that figure rises to 43 percent. Eleven African nations, including the DRC, use French as their only official language. Another nine African countries have French and one other language as their official tongues. Still others have a significant francophone, or French-speaking, populations.

The French language came to Africa with colonialism in the late nineteenth century. In what has come to be called the "Scramble for Africa," the European powers rushed to grab up lands on the continent so as to extend their empires. This phase, between 1881 and 1914, saw seven European countries impose colonial rule over 90 percent of Africa, with mostly only Ethiopia remaining independent.

France took over large portions of northwestern Africa, but Belgium conquered the Congo early on. King Leopold II of Belgium established the Congo Free State, and his extraordinarily brutal treatment of the Congolese people is well known and well documented. Today, Belgium is a country with three official languages—French, Dutch, and German—but at the time, French was the language of the Belgian authorities, and so it became the language of the Congo.

Today, some 120 million Africans speak French, making Africa the continent with the most French speakers in the world. Over time, naturally, the language acquired many regional variations—some of which vary from standard French quite a bit. They have incorporated regional African vocabulary, intonation, and pronunciation. In Kinshasa, the second largest francophone city in the world after Paris, the French is further influenced by Belgian French, which has its own idiosyncrasies.

In Kinshasa and other parts of the Congo, code switching is a common linguistic practice. That is the habit of verbally switching between two languages in one conversation, or even one sentence. In Kinshasa, for example, it would be typical to hear people using both Lingala and French at the same time.

all rivers." Since the sixteenth century, the river has been known at various times as either the Zaire or the Congo, with Zaire generally being more common in French and Portuguese and Congo being more common in English.

The currency was also called the zaire, and so were the local cigarettes and gasoline. Naming the money after the country's most vital geographic element has some interesting parallels—in South Africa the currency is the rand, the common name for the gold-mining area of the Witwatersrand, while in Botswana the currency is the *pula*, meaning "rain," something more precious than gold. Today, the DRC's currency is the Congolese franc (CDF).

The country underwent many name changes. The Republic of the Belgian Congo became the Federal Republic of the Congo upon independence. After Mobutu seized power in 1965, it was the Democratic Republic of the Congo, then in 1971 the Republic of Zaire. In 1997 President Laurent Kabila restored the DRC name.

GREETINGS

"Peace be unto you" is followed by courteous inquiries about the family and the person's health and prosperity. The answer is always that things are fine, "Thanks be to God." It would be exceedingly bad manners to talk business without a proper greeting.

The most common greeting is the Swahili "*Jambo!*" (YAM-boh), or "Hello," to which the reply is "*Jambo-sana!*" (YAM-boh SAH-nah), or "Hello very much!" In Lingala, the greeting is "*Mbote*" (m-BOH-tay), and in Nandé, "*Wavuskiry*" (wah-voos-KEE-ray).

INTERNET LINKS

http://www.bbc.co.uk/languages/other/swahili/guide/facts.shtml
The BBC presents ten fun facts about the Swahili language.

https://www.omniglot.com/writing/lingala.htm
Omniglot gives an introduction to the Lingala language.

https://www.omniglot.com/writing/swahili.htm
An introduction to Swahili with audio files and videos.

ARTS

A violin maker poses in his workshop in Kinshasa.

10

"SURVIVAL FUELS CREATIVITY," SAYS A member of the innovative Congolese electronic music group KOKOKO! He and his bandmates make hypnotic dance music using electronic instruments they have invented using junk gathered from the streets. These include an old fashioned typewriter rigged to bang on a piece of scrap metal as the player types, a harp made of wires strung to old coffee cans, bottles of water pitched to play melodies, and a ghetto talk box made from a car cassette player. From those found objects, the band produces sublime music that has caught the attention of fans far beyond the borders of Kinshasa, its hometown.

"Survival fuels creativity" could be a motto for much of Congolese art, and may also explain the highly creative work being done in this very poor country today. The tongue-in-cheek Western notion of the "starving artist" is closer to the naked truth here, but that doesn't stop many artists from pursuing their passion—particularly in music.

For decades, Kinshasa was the music capital of Africa. In the 1950s and 1960s, it had a vibrant recording industry; but over the years, ongoing turmoil forced much of the music scene to move to Paris and elsewhere. In Kinshasa today, there are almost no event organizers, investors, or professionals. The city lacks venues and support facilities such as sound and equipment renting companies. Nevertheless, live music thrives in bars, night clubs, and on the streets.

Given the dire state of the nation, it might be surprising to discover that Congolese music is often quite joyful and uplifting. Or perhaps it's not so surprising. The music can be intensely freeing, offering a sort of transcendent lifeline to its fans.

The depths of poverty in Congo, however, have also led to a practice called *mabanga*. In some ways, it's just another example of survival-fueled creativity; though in this case, a resourceful way of making money. Popular artists accept money from politicians or other wealthy, powerful people to include their names, or the names of their family members, in a song's lyrics. This musical name-dropping, called shout-outs, can be thought of as a form of campaign or business ad that some musicians shrug off. To them it's just another form of selling their work. But others think it's a sellout. Critics find it a disturbing and corrupting imposition on the free spirit of art itself.

MUSIC AND DANCE

Music and dance go together in the Congo, in both the traditional and contemporary styles. Nobody can listen to music without clapping, stamping, singing, or dancing to the rhythm. Usually there will be a drum of some shape and an assortment of other percussion instruments such as rattles, bells, a

Villagers greet visiting **UNICEF** doctors with song and dance.

MUSIC WITH A BEAT

The pounding beat of much of modern pop music has its origin in Africa. There is a Latin-American influence too, which results in a music similar to rumba music. This style was introduced when radio stations played music by the early Cuban rumba bands. Local groups imitated the rhythm, often playing in what were called Congo bars. A guitar was often accompanied by some lively brass instruments. The beat was provided by drums, rattles, or even bottles struck to produce a particular note.

With the arrival of the acoustic guitar and electric amplifiers, the bands became larger and more successful. European jazz was added to the mix, and eventually, American rap and hip-hop added even more complexity. The ability to improvise with whatever instruments were available, combined with an appreciation of the complex African rhythms, created Afropop and many other new African music genres.

wooden xylophone, and resonant blocks. In ritual dances there is sometimes a particular drumbeat associated with each ancestral spirit or power involved. The drummer must know each special rhythm.

Traditional dance is usually part of a social ritual or festive celebration. For example, the Salampasu people of Kasai Province are proud that they were once fierce warriors renowned for beheading their enemies. The men, dressed in fiber costumes adorned with leopard skins, perform wild masked dances in which they brandish fearsome looking swords to maintain their reputation. The Kuba dancers perform to give regal status to their royal masks, so their dances are a sequence of complex routines presented with great dignity. Part of their costume is a huge feather crest with red interwoven ribbons. Near the eastern Great Rift Valley lakes, it is the initiation dances that predominate. Boys and girls aged ten to twelve paint white spots on their bodies and perform dances with elaborate girdles of cloth and beads, all as part of their initiation from childhood to maturity.

The *kalimba* (ka-LIM-bah), a sort of thumb piano with hand-plucked metal strips set against a wooden soundboard, is heard everywhere. The Congolese also love local village music from flutes made of wood or reed. Panpipes, horns, and single-string resonators are popular, too.

"The King of Rumba Rock" Papa Wemba (1949–2016) was one of Africa's most popular musicians. He started out singing with a Congolese rumba band in 1969, and was instrumental in the development of soukous *(derived from the French word* secouer, *"to shake"), a genre of rumba-derived dance music which incorporates syncopated rhythms and intricate, electric guitar melodies. In 1977, he formed his band Viva La Musica, which over time evolved from a soukous band into a "world music" group, merging Central African musical traditions with Western pop, rock, and rap. The band eventually moved*

to Paris, where Wemba collaborated with a wide range of international musicians. He worked on more than thirty-five albums, many of them big hits.

More than just a musician, Papa Wemba was also a leading arbiter of fashion as a founder of the sapeur *movement. The group promoted high standards of grooming and elegant attire.*

Although he achieved some international recognition in world music circles, especially in Europe, Papa Wemba was primarily a star in Africa. In 2016, he collapsed onstage during a concert in Ivory Coast, and died at the age of sixty-six.

The DRC has blended its indigenous musical sources with Caribbean rumba and merengue music to give birth to *soukous*, a type of dance music. Many Congolese bands sing in Lingala, one of the main languages of the DRC.

TRADITIONAL ARTS

Deeply rooted in the culture, the indigenous arts are (or were) used for ceremonial occasions or for everyday activities such as singing, dancing, and storytelling. They often have a mix of magical and religious significance. Wood carvings are some of the most striking examples of African art. Various themes are clear in the art of the Congo region, whether ancient or modern.

One is the eternal struggle between the forces of order and control and the wild, uncontrolled chaos that threatens from outside. For example, the masks worn at the start of the initiation rites for Congolese boys are made of rough materials, while those worn at the end are of carved wood with more human faces, signifying initiation into civilized society. Masks served to protect the common people from the power of those who wore them—the king or the priest—and to echo the characters of the creatures who lived around them.

Wooden masks and figurines carved in the traditional style are exhibited for sale.

TRIBAL SPECIALTIES

Individual art styles are influenced by the materials available, by lifestyle, and by the culture of the artist.

In the rain forests of the northern region, the Komo people create wooden masks, weapons, and fetishes. A style emerged here, possibly brought by migrants from Nigeria, of a heart-shaped face mask, with the two eye sockets at the broader top and a chin and a mouth at the narrower base. Much of the Komo craftwork is associated with the rituals of their soothsayers or healers, who are adorned with feathers, bark belts, ivory bracelets, and little

The belief that an inanimate object can hold special power of its own is particularly strong in Africa. The fetish is often carved in human form, though it may be merely a bone, a tooth, or a piece of fur. People believe that a fetish was given some power by a person skilled in traditional sorcery or that it acquired an ability to ward off evil spirits or bad luck. To call a fetish a good luck charm is to underrate the importance attached to such an object. The Kongo people carve many fetishes, usually animals or devilish-looking human figures, into which nails are stuck, apparently to increase the potency of their magic.

bells hanging from armbands. On the edge of the forest, the Mangbetu, of Sudanese origin, wear hardly any clothing in their ritual dances but instead paint the whole body in elaborate geometric patterns and braid their hair into a tall wickerwork frame stuck together with ivory or wooden pins.

The people of the lower reaches of the Congo River were influenced by the Portuguese, who introduced Christianity. Some Christian visual signs were adopted and given an African symbolism. In Kongowood carving, admired for its realism and relatively relaxed poses of the human figures, the cross or the crucifix is a symbol of power.

From the Pende people, east of Kinshasa, come wooden masks with distinctive, heavy-lidded eyes and grotesque features—features admired and copied by Picasso in the years after 1906. The Pende also weave fawn- and black-striped coverings for the whole body from raffia, leaves, and feathers; these are used by dancers in circumcision rituals. Since the Pende carvers are considered to have special powers and are thus respected in their villages, onlookers are fearful of the dancers as well, as if they too have taken on some unknown spirit power.

The savanna region of Kasai is home to such old tribes as the Luba and the Kuba. Luba masks were the first Central African art to be recognized internationally. Their now well-known, hemispherical masks have protruding eyes and exaggerated nose and mouth features, sometimes painted black with white parallel lines. Few of those on sale in the street markets are Luba carvings; they are backstreet copies made anywhere in West or Central

Africa. Anything original and genuinely old is safe in a museum, such as the Académie des Beaux-Arts in Kinshasa.

The Kuba, like the Kongo, once had a powerful kingdom. Much of their craftwork was developed to please or adorn royalty, and carving became a much-respected art form. One carver in each reign was given the honor of carving a statue of the king, who dressed in sumptuous costumes and wore royal masks shaped like helmets with the face covered by leopard skin, decorated with beads and cowries, and crowned with a crest of eagle feathers. Even today, some traditional masks may be worn only by those of the royal line. The Kuba style is highly decorative with many geometric patterns. Kuba artisans create a variety of objects: wooden cups, ornate boxes, game boards, drums, pipes, stools, and fancy spoons.

PAINTING

Paint is expensive, so it needs to have a practical use. Advertising is an obvious one. Congolese artists paint on the walls of buildings using ordinary commercial paint in bright colors, mostly in the flat style of folk art. They choose themes that will attract customers. For hairdressers they paint the range of ladies' hairstyles. A café may have pictures of favorite musicians or sports stars.

Many artists struggling to make a living in Kinshasa prefer to paint scenes with some sort of social significance. They see themselves as commentators or critics of the world around them.

Chéri Samba, an internationally known Congolese artist, paints portraits, usually from photographs, and wall signs. He likes to include some social or political message on issues such as drug addiction, abuse of power, bribery, and AIDS, but also enjoys including the comical side of life.

Kasongo (many Congolese prefer to be known by one name only) concentrates on paintings of the violence and cruelty that erupted when Belgian paratroopers took the city of Lubumbashi in 1964. He shows the brutal beatings of civilians fleeing from a pipe smoking figure representing Henry Stanley, the symbol of colonization.

The venerable Kalume is gentler-minded. He creates wall paintings of

rivers and landscapes, often with a religious significance.

In a lighter mood, Sim Simaro likes to paint buses. Since he enjoys traveling himself, he details all sorts of transportation problems, providing scenes of life in Kinshasa today.

CARVING

Wood is the most readily available material in the Congo region, so most of the craftwork offered to tourists or exhibited in the country's few museums are highly polished wood carvings.

A woman in Makwatsha decorates a house wall.

Masks, known generally as *mbuya*, are by far the most common. Some masks bear the scarification marks peculiar to a tribe, such as the body patterns of the Bena Lulua or the Mangbetu of the northeast. The masks made by the Bapuma people copy the cuts they make on the forehead between the eyes and on the temples. These masks usually have a cloth attached that completely encloses the dancer, who often performs on stilts.

Beads are used to create objects such as necklaces, bangles, and headdresses, which by their patterns and colors represent spiritual values vital to the community. Such items play major roles in community rituals such as birth, circumcision, marriage, and death. Other craft items include boxes, carved doors, necklaces made of copper or shells, and dark green malachite jewelry from the southern Katanga region. There is very little carved from ivory, and most metalwork tends to be for daily use rather than decorative.

**http://www.aljazeera.com/indepth/features/2017/05/congo-artists
-rely-patronage-wealthy-170529092655899.html**
This article discusses the practice of mabanga in Congolese music.

http://www.bbc.com/news/entertainment-arts-36123966
This obituary for Papa Wemba includes a photo collection and a video
clip of his music.

**https://www.britannica.com/place/Democratic-Republic-of-the
-Congo/The-arts**
This entry provides a quick overview of the arts in the Congo.

**https://www.nytimes.com/2015/07/25/arts/design/exploring-a
-century-of-art-from-congo.html**
This review of an art exhibit in Paris shows examples of contemporary
Congolese art.

**http://www.thecitizen.co.tz/magazine/thebeat/The-beautiful
-Congolese-world-of-Rumba-music/1843792-3973390-1lgif6
/index.html**
This article gives a quick history of Congolese rumba.

**https://theculturetrip.com/africa/dr-congo/articles/top-10
-congolese-bands-musicians-you-should-know/**
This site presents ten Congolese music greats, from Papa Wemba to
Fally Ipupa.

LEISURE

Men play mankala with smooth black pebbles.

11

M OST CONGOLESE DO NOT HAVE the luxury of indulging in any kind of organized leisure activity. For those who work daily to grow food at subsistence level, there is no leisure time.

However, one can still see children playing on the streets or adults enjoying a game of mankala. Congolese love soccer and are avid supporters of their national team. Many children see their soccer players as heroes. Other leisure activities that the Congolese engage in are storytelling and dancing. The weekly break from work for many is attendance at church, when everyone wears his or her best clothes.

Congolese youngsters play mostly in imitation of adults. Girls practice carrying loads on their head and play "making families." Boys make their own bows and arrows to practice hunting and are wildly excited if they return home with a kill. They climb trees and run races. And always, everywhere, the boys play soccer. The ball may be a bundle of rags tied with coarse string or a cheap plastic ball from the market, but children will make it work.

MANKALA

Mankala, or mancala, (man-KAH-la) is a game similar to backgammon and is played with regional variations all over Africa. In Congo it is called *bao* by those who speak Swahili. It supposedly originated in Egypt thousands of years ago. Usually two people play, although teams can play taking turns. Above all, it requires time.

The board consists of two rows of six cups or, more simply, holes in the ground. To start, four beans—or pebbles or marbles or dried peas—

Born in Kinshasa in 1966, Dikembe Mutombo is the seventh of ten children born to Samuel and the late Biamba Marie Mutombo. He arrived in the United States in 1987 on an academic scholarship to attend Georgetown University in Washington, DC. As a premed major, he dreamed of becoming a doctor and returning to the DRC to practice medicine.

In his second year at Georgetown, coach John Thompson invited Mutombo, who is 7 feet 2 inches (218 cm) tall, to try out for the university's renowned basketball team. After joining the team, Mutombo redirected his academic ambitions and graduated from Georgetown with dual degrees in linguistics and diplomacy. Mutombo is fluent in nine languages, including five African languages. Following graduation he played for a number of NBA teams and is an eight-time NBA All-Star. He retired in 2009. In 2015 he was inducted into the Naismith Memorial Basketball Hall of Fame.

In his post-basketball career, Mutombo has dedicated himself to humanitarian work, for which his has been awarded many honors. But that interest did not begin with his retirement. Mutombo has long been dedicated to improving the health, education, and quality of life of the people in his native country. Among other projects, he built the Biamba Marie Mutombo Hospital in Kinshasa, which opened in 2007. He named it for his mother, who died in 1997 when fighting in his parents' city prevented his father from being able to get her to a hospital when she fell ill.

are placed in each cup. The first player takes all the beans from any cup on his side of the board and drops them one at a time in each neighboring cup to the right—in other words, moving counterclockwise around the board. When the last bean dropped falls into a cup on his opponent's side that contains only one or two beans, he gets to take those beans.

The basic idea is to strategize in such a way as to make this happen, but there are regional variations, and only a mankala player can explain them fully. The result is a game as complex and absorbing as chess. Village players may be unable to read or write, but they can outthink any visitor at mankala.

SPORTS

If the national game is mankala, the national sport is soccer. The DRC is as soccer crazy as any other country in Africa. President Mobutu was fiercely proud of Les Léopards (the Leopards), the national team. While the rebel forces were fighting their way across the country, the national soccer team still played its qualifying matches in the World Cup, and the players were national heroes far more popular than any politician.

Barefoot boys play soccer in Lubumbashi, in the country's mining district.

In January 2018, FIFA (the world governing body for soccer) ranked the DRC number 43 in the world and number 5 among African countries. A number of Congolese athletes, particularly soccer players, play professionally in other countries.

In Kinshasa there is an impressive stadium that Mobutu built to host the 1974 world heavyweight championship fight between the American boxers Muhammad Ali and George Foreman—remembered in boxing history as the "Rumble in the Jungle." He considered both fighters to be "sons of Africa" and was proud that the first such championship in Africa should be in Zaire.

STORYTELLING

Storytelling is a popular pastime in the Congo. The traditional folklore story conveys some piece of wisdom or social advice through a simple, often magical tale. The storyteller is usually elderly and respected, with the skill to create different characters with his voice and the noises of jungle animals as well if required. One favorite tale is the story of the Creator god and his four children: Raffia-palm, Liana, Wine-palm, and Oil-palm, his favorite.

In modern times a new kind of storytelling has emerged. Instead of traditional folklore around the fire at night, there is a call for modern stories for adults. In a bar or a café, someone known as a good storyteller will be persuaded to tell a tale from the recent troubled history or a legend

THE THREE BROTHERS: A CONGOLESE FOLKTALE

In the beginning, when KaCongo* had still one mother and the whole family yet lived on grass and roots and knew not how to plant, a woman brought forth three babes in one birth.

"Oh, what am I to do with them?" she cried. "I do not want them; I will leave them here in the grass." And the three little ones were very hungry, and looked about them for food. They walked and walked a long, long way, until at last they came to a river, which they crossed.

They saw bananas, and palm-trees, and mandioca growing in great quantities, but dared not eat the fruit thereof. Then the river-spirit called to them and told them to eat of these good things. And the tiniest of the three tried a banana and found it very sweet. Then the other two ate them and found them very good. And after this, they ate of the other trees and so grew up well nurtured and strong, and they learnt how to become carpenters and blacksmiths, and built themselves houses. The river-spirit supplied them with women for wives, and soon they multiplied and created a town of their own.

A man who had wandered far from his town came near to where the three brothers had built their home and was astonished, as he approached it, to hear voices. This man happened to be the father of the three brothers.

So he returned to his town, without having entered the village, to tell his wife that he had found her children. Then the old woman set out with her husband to seek for her children, and wandered and wandered on, until she was too tired to go any further when she sank down by the wayside to rest.

Now one of the children of the three brothers came across the old woman, and was afraid, and ran back to tell his father.

Then the three brothers set out with the intention of killing the intruder, but the river-spirit called out to them, and told them not to kill her, but to take her to their home, and feed her, for she was their mother. And they did so.

*KaCongo (KaKongo) was an early kingdom on the Atlantic coast at the mouth the Congo River. In this story, it is probably a reference to the ancient Congo region.

of unworthy politicians. The teller may stop partway through the story and refuse to finish unless more tobacco or beer is provided.

NIGHTLIFE

The Congolese love dancing, and they do it in a frenzied fashion. What the Kinshasans call *kwasa kwasa* (KWA-sa KWA-sa) is the favorite. In the old Cité district of Kinshasa, there are open-air roadside gigs, rooftop terraces, underground dives, and dance places.

Bars that offer dancing as well as drinking are known as *ngandas* (un-GAN-dahs). Nightclubs have theatrical lighting and floor shows, charge astronomical prices, and provide military-style doormen. Though some establishments stay open until midnight, most customers leave by 9 p.m. for fear of late night robbers.

INTERNET LINKS

http://www.magx.com/people/everyday-life-in-democratic-republic-of-congo.html
These photos present glimpses of everyday life in the DRC.

https://www.thespruce.com/mancala-411837
This site provides the rules of and a bit of history about mankala.

https://theundefeated.com/features/dikembe-mutombo-nba-africa-basketball-without-borders
This interview with Dikembe Mutombo highlights his work with Basketball Without Borders

FESTIVALS

12

MOST CONGOLESE FESTIVALS ARE relatively quiet affairs. Indeed many people there may wonder at the meaning of public festivals, as there seems precious little to celebrate. There are no grand cultural events and no street parades, apart from patriotic marches. More common are smaller scale festivals focused on the family.

As in most countries, the calendar of annual holidays in the Democratic Republic of the Congo includes both national commemorations of the state and religious festivals.

PATRIOTIC HOLIDAYS

National state holidays observe important days in the history of the nation. January 4, Day of the Martyrs for Independence, honors those who died in the uprising against the Belgian colonial regime on January 4, 1959. Liberation Day, May 17, marks the 1997 coup d'état led by Laurent Kabila against Mobutu Sese Seko. Independence Day, June 30, commemorates the 1960 break from colonialism. Heroes' Day is a two-day commemoration of the assassinations of the revered leaders Laurent Kabila and Patrice Lumumba.

Zaire Day, which was once a celebration of the nation itself, has been removed from the calendar. Mobutu used both holidays for military parades and a show of power. The flag would be ceremoniously raised

The DRC doesn't observe Mothers Day or Fathers Day, but instead celebrates Parents Day, usually August 1. In addition to honoring parents, the holiday is a time to pay tribute to grandparents, aunts, uncles, and other family members involved in the upbringing of the children. In the morning, Congolese families will visit cemeteries to clean and decorate the graves of deceased relatives.

and the national anthem sung. The anthem during Mobutu's time was *"Zaïrois, dans la paix retrouvée, peuple uni, nous sommes zaïrois"* ("Zaireans, in peace found again, a united people, we are Zaireans"). After Mobutu's era ended, the country went back to its pre-Zaire anthem, *"Debout Congolaise"* ("Arise Congolese").

Congolese national holidays and parades are accompanied by flag waving. The country has had seven flags in the past hundred years or so. The first flag of the independent Congo was light blue with a gold five-point star in the center and six smaller stars down the left edge. In 1971 Mobutu created a green flag with a yellow circle in the middle showing a dark brown hand waving the flaming red torch of freedom. Kabila's alliance reintroduced the original flag of independent Congo, except that the field was dark blue.

After the new constitution was adopted in 2006, the flag was changed to one with a sky-blue background, a yellow star in the upper left corner, and a diagonal red stripe with a yellow band down the middle. The blue represents peace and hope; red, the blood of the country's martyrs: and yellow, the country's wealth and prosperity. The star symbolizes unity and the brilliant future for the country.

RELIGIOUS DAYS

The main feast days of the Roman Catholic Church are Christmas (the birth of Jesus), Lent (his temptations in the wilderness), Good Friday and Easter (the Crucifixion and Resurrection), and Whitsunday (which celebrates Pentecost, the descent of the Holy Spirit). The actual calendar days of these celebrations vary from year to year. Depending on the resources available, there may be special services of Mass with communion and processions. The same religious festivals are observed by the Protestant churches, though usually with less ceremony.

For Congolese Christian families, religious holidays are special days; they wear their best clothes to church and gather to sing songs in a communal celebration. On Christmas, those who can will cook a special family dinner and present small gifts. New clothes are often the main Christmas gift for children.

Christmas and New Year's Day are celebrated in most African countries, but Mobutu, as part of his Africanization program, tried to minimize the influence of the Catholic Church. In 1974 Mobutu banned Christmas celebrations and declared that it would no longer be a Zairian holiday. He also banned religious instruction from the schools, and ordered crucifixes and pictures of the pope removed from schools, hospitals, and public buildings; the removed items were replaced by pictures of President Mobutu himself.

FAMILY EVENTS

The most important festivities and gatherings are family celebrations such as weddings, baptisms, and funerals. For the Congolese, there are speeches, drinking, and singing and dancing for happy occasions. Guests at a baptism are expected to bring a gift for both proud parents; money is quite acceptable. After the church service, there is a celebratory meal.

The traditional celebrations for a wedding are so expensive that many men cannot afford to get married until later in life. Before the wedding itself, there is up to a week of parties, visits to relatives, and exchanging of gifts of money or livestock. After the ceremony, held in a church or at the mayor's office, close friends and relations go to a suitable house for the final round of eating and dancing. Presents from the groom to the bride's family may cost the equivalent of several hundred dollars—an astronomical sum for a man whose annual income may be less than $200.

Funerals are more solemn events. The Congolese believe in burying their dead. There is no thought of cremation. Burial is a sacred duty to the deceased, who is now one of the revered ancestors.

INTERNET LINK

https://www.timeanddate.com/holidays/dr-congo
This site lists the public holidays and observances in Congo.

FOOD

A happy woman displays a bowl of insect larvae for a
protein-filled snack.

13

I N SOME PARTS OF THE WORLD, PEOPLE eat foods that many in the United States consider exotic, disgusting, uncivilized, or morally wrong. In Europe, for example, some people eat horse meat; in parts of Asia, some folks eat dog meat; and in Iceland, it was once perfectly normal to eat whale meat. In all of these cases, the tide of popular opinion is turning against such practices, and they are no longer common.

Throughout history, human beings have eaten what Mother Nature provided, and regional cuisines developed accordingly. It's only recently that people have been able to obtain foods from other parts of the world, in any season, and store them safely for eating at a later time.

Today, there are a number of reasons to scorn the eating of certain animals. Some objections are based on the nature of a given species' relationship with humans. Animals kept as pets, such as dogs, cats, horses, or even guinea pigs—which are eaten in some parts of South America—are often considered morally off-limits to human consumption. On the other hand, domesticated animals such as cows, chickens, and sheep, can straddle the line between pet and meat source, blurring the distinction. Some people choose not to eat animals at all. In sufficiently wealthy cultures, it's not necessary to eat meat for health purposes, and vegetarianism is a viable option as long as people are careful to find their proteins from plant-based sources.

The oil palm is a favorite tree of the Congolese. It is a most valuable cash crop, and no cooking is complete without palm oil, which they say "strokes the stomach." Palm oil is also used as a traditional medicine against scabies and for making margarine and soap.

A child carries a basket containing a large rat and a monkey arm for a family meal.

In the case of whale meat, which provided sustenance for northern peoples for centuries, or shark fins, which are cultural delicacies in China, it's a question of protecting endangered species. People no longer need to eat whales to stay alive. And the controversy over the harvesting of shark fins, which provide no particular nutritive value, is another story altogether.

Other animals, such as rodents and snakes, are considered unpalatable in many countries, but the reasons are primarily cultural. What is gross to one person may be delicious to another. In other words, making negative judgments about the cuisines of other countries can be a form of cultural condescension. Conversely, in the interest of preserving species, it may be time for certain cultural traditions to be abandoned.

However, in Central Africa—particularly in the Congo—the matter of "inappropriate" food is far more complicated and urgent. In fact, it is a crisis of many dimensions.

HUNGER

The DRC is one of the poorest countries on earth. The vast majority of its people are underfed and suffering from poor health as a result of an insufficiently nutritious diet. The already terrible situation there has been made worse by on-going conflicts, particularly in the eastern part of the country.

In 2017, the UN's World Food Programme (WFP) and the UN Food and Agriculture Organization (FAO), along with other humanitarian groups, warned that the country was on the brink of famine. The UN's criteria for famine are: at least 20 percent of households in an area face extreme food shortages with a limited ability to cope; the prevalence of acute malnutrition in children exceeds 30 percent; and the death rate exceeds two persons per 10,000 persons per day. Famines can develop as a result of natural devastation, such as crop failures three years in a row, but more often they are brought about by human-imposed hardship, usually of a political nature, such as war or genocide.

Between June 2016 and June 2017, the number of Congolese living at pre-famine levels of food insecurity and requiring urgent humanitarian assistance rose from 5.9 million to 7.7 million—a 30 percent increase in one year—according to the UN food agencies. In rural areas, hunger is particularly pervasive, and one-tenth of the people experience acute hunger.

The Congolese eat what they can gather or grow. The Congolese will cook and eat tree-living grubs, monitor lizards, bats, and rats. Almost anything will go into the stew pot that simmers on an open fire or a wood-burning stove. To Westerners, such a diet might indicate desperation; the Congolese, on the other hand, appreciate the bountiful diversity of food from nature.

MALNOURISHED CHILDREN

Children suffer the most from insufficient nutrition because the damage to brain and bodily development can be irreversible even after improving the diet. If all of a Congolese mother's children survive beyond the age of five, she considers herself fortunate. UNICEF reports that in 2016, the under five mortality rate in Congo was 94 deaths per 1,000 children under five. This figure is among the highest in the world, but is a great improvement over only a few years ago.

The idea of providing children with a balanced diet is unfamiliar to many parents and often impossible in any event. According to a 2017 FAO report, 43 percent of Congolese children under five years old suffer chronic malnutrition, and those figures are higher in the violence-torn eastern provinces of North and South Kivu and Kasaï. These children develop a protein deficiency usually known by its Ghanaian name, *kwashiorkor*, which stunts growth and causes the muscles to waste away.

A nurse from Scotland weighs a baby in Dubie, in Katanga province. Her T-shirt identifies her as being with Médecins Sans Frontières (Doctors Without Borders).

In Kasala, Congolese women carry heavy sacks of food on their heads.

FOOD SUPPLY CHALLENGES

Wars and conflict increase food insecurity because they force people to flee from their homes, leaving their crops to wither and their livestock to starve. Conflict destroys agricultural infrastructure and disrupts markets. Displaced people settle in refugee camps, where they are susceptible to filth, starvation, and disease. Wars also make it difficult and dangerous for governments and international agencies to get food and medical relief to the people who need it.

After conflict erupted in Kasaï province in August 2016, for example, some 1.4 million people fled their homes. By 2018, most of those families had missed two consecutive planting seasons. Many of the starving people eat little more than a meal a day—typically just cassava root and leaves. Such a diet lacks protein, vitamins, and minerals. When people resort to eating seeds that should be planted, as some do, they impact their ability to grow food in the future.

In Africa, the forest is often referred to as "the bush" and the meat from wildlife is called "bushmeat." Crocodiles, monkeys, antelopes, squirrels, porcupines, and even elephants, gorillas, and chimpanzees are hunted for food. In rural areas of the Congo basin, people get up to 60 or 80 percent of their protein from bushmeat. The rest comes from fish, grubs, caterpillars, or whatever they can find. There is little or no livestock.

A significant uptick in bushmeat hunting resulted after mining and logging companies cleared roads into the dense forests back in the 1980s. Animals that had previously been protected by the impenetrable jungles were now accessible, and this has led to the increased endangerment of certain vulnerable species, such as gorillas and elephants. The concept of protecting endangered species can draw little sympathy or understanding from impoverished people. Guards in national parks face a constant threat of violence from angry villagers and poachers.

Not all bushmeat animals are endangered, however. Rodents make up a large percentage of the catch, and their populations are rather resilient to the pressures of hunting.

Aside from animal conservation issues, there is also a very real danger to people who eat bushmeat. Most don't realize that certain deadly diseases can be transmitted by handling, cutting the flesh, cooking, and eating certain kinds of wild animals—particularly animals that are genetically close to humans, such as chimpanzees, gorillas and bonobos. The Ebola virus and HIV, the virus that causes AIDS, are two examples that are thought to have jumped from simians to humans this way. Gorillas may carry diseases such as simian foamy virus, chickenpox, tuberculosis, measles, rubella, yellow fever, and yaws. People have caught such diseases, and some died. Even eating the meat of African squirrels may be dangerous. It's thought to be a source of the monkeypox virus that has infected people in the DRC.

It's not just the poor who are eating bushmeat. Among Africa's wealthy elite, the meat of apes and elephants can be considered prestigious delicacies to be served at fancy banquets, and seen as a way of celebrating African culture.

Even in areas not affected by conflict, hunger is a constant factor because of severe poverty. Farmers do not have the money, equipment, or knowledge to employ modern agricultural methods, so crop results are much lower than they could be. Poverty and tradition combine to send people in search of whatever food they can find. Often, that food is bushmeat.

EVERYDAY FARE

The main meal, eaten in the evening, consists of a filling staple food such as rice or cassava, with a bowl of sauce for extra taste, and perhaps some vegetables, fish, or meat. These protein foods flavor the meal; they are not the main items as in a Western diet. In many parts of the DRC, more fish is eaten than meat. Of the staple foods, rice is the most common and the most popular, but it is also the most expensive because nearly all rice is imported.

Cassava is common and cheap; when cooked it makes a sticky white mush called *fufu*. Bananas are sometimes mixed with mashed plantains or cassava. Young green okra pods, also called gumbo, are used as a staple vegetable. The

A poacher sells dead monkeys on the side of the road.

CASSAVA

The most common staple food in the country is cassava (also called manioc), which is filling but has limited nutritional value. Many malnourished children owe their lack of

growth to a diet of cassava (in the form of fufu) and little else. The Congolese make flour from its tuberous roots and cook it into a starchy gruel. Dried, ground cassava makes a sort of flour known as farine de manioc *(fah-REEN duh MAN-ee-oh), which can be stored. Before cooking it needs to be soaked in salted water, which causes it to swell to about double its size. The Congolese also soak cassava leaves in boiling water to remove the acetic acid, then pound them to a pulp and cook them with palm oil to produce a green vegetable that resembles spinach. Fermented cassava is used to make an alcoholic drink. In Western countries, cassava powder is better known as tapioca, a thickening agent used in pies and puddings.*

Congolese enjoy their food spicy hot, though they also have a milder peanut-based sauce.

The meats available include almost anything from the woodland, as well as chickens, the occasional duck or goose, or, for those who can afford it, the rare treat of beef. The Congolese are particularly fond of eating monkey but will happily feast on porcupine, crocodile, or antelope. Pigeons, rats, locusts, and mopane worms are on the menu when available. If they kill an elephant or a chimpanzee for food, they smoke-cure the meat to preserve it, but also to disguise it; these animals are listed as endangered species, and the hunter could be fined.

Fruit is eaten often, although a dessert course is unusual. Bananas are popular, cooked or raw. Virtually all other tropical fruits are available:

pineapples, papayas, avocados, oranges, and coconuts.

A typical meal in a rural household—the only meal of the day in many homes—is served from a bowl on the ground. Those eating the meal wash their hands first and usually take off their shoes before sitting on the mats. They eat with the right hand, often tucking the left hand behind the back. Each person takes a small handful of the rice or cassava, dips it into the sauce or the meat, forms it into a ball, and then eats it. Visitors are served first by the head of the household. After the meal, a washbasin is passed around.

Breakfast and lunch may be dry cakes of cassava or some fruit. The cooked meal comes in the early evening. Freshwater fish is eaten by many; a favorite is grilled perch, or *capitaine* (KAP-ee-TAYN). A family living close to the river will salt and dry any spare fish to preserve them, since few homes have electricity, and even fewer have refrigerators. Long-brewed herbal tea is an inexpensive and refreshing drink. The Congolese use various leaves such as lemongrass to flavor the tea.

Fishermen lower fish traps into the rapids on the Congo River in Kisangani.

EATING OUT

In Kinshasa there are Italian, Greek, Chinese, French, and Portuguese restaurants. Even more popular are those offering African dishes such as cassava leaf stew, known as *sakasaka,* and wild game, or *gibier* (JEE-bee-ay), all served with rice. Menus might include wild pig (which tastes like tough pork), impala (similar to venison), or snake (salty and bony).

When available, the favorite poultry is guinea fowl, which has a darker, stronger-tasting flesh than chicken. There might be roast fish flavored with hot chili and served with cassava porridge. A popular dish is *moambé* (MWAM-bay), rice with a spicy sauce of peanuts and palm oil served usually with chicken, though sometimes with fish. Kinshasa residents enjoy cream-filled cakes and pastries as well as ice cream. Bitter cola nuts, used as an appetite suppressant, and fresh fruit such as pineapple are always available.

The more common method of eating out is to buy from the street-corner cooks who sell fried sweet potatoes, grilled skewers of unidentifiable meat, or *pidi-pidi* (PEE-dee PEE-dee)—sausages made of crushed peanuts and cassava, fried in palm oil and covered with spices. In the eastern towns vendors cook bananas in melted butter and roll them in chopped peanuts.

A couple share a drink and a bit to eat at a bar in Kinshasa.

INTERNET LINKS

https://news.mongabay.com/2017/07/african-great-ape-bushmeat-crisis-intensifies-few-solutions-in-sight
This shocking article provides in-depth information about the bushmeat crisis in Central Africa.

https://www.theguardian.com/environment/2010/sep/07/congo-chimpanzees-bushmeat
This article focuses on the threat to chimpanzees being killed for bushmeat in the DRC.

http://www.travelingeast.com/africa/democratic-republic-of-congo/congolese-cuisine
Some typical foods of the Congo are highlighted on this site.

POULET À LA MOAMBÉ
(CHICKEN GROUNDNUT OR PEANUT STEW)

This dish is often called the national dish of the Congo. Authentically, it is made with palm oil or butter (*moambé*)—but you can substitute peanut oil or any cooking oil—and homemade peanut butter. A coarse-ground natural-style peanut butter will approximate the result. It is often served with *fufu*, but white rice is a good alternative. Variations include adding cut-up eggplant, yams, or greens to the stew.

3-pound (1.36 kg) boiler/fryer chicken,
   cut into serving pieces
1 teaspoon salt
3 tablespoons palm or peanut oil (or any
   cooking oil)
1 Tbsp. butter
1 onion, minced
2 cloves garlic, minced
½ tsp ground nutmeg
½ tsp cayenne pepper
2 cups (450 grams) canned tomato sauce
1 cup (240 mL) water or chicken broth
1 cup (250 g) natural-style peanut butter
White rice or fufu.

Season the chicken with the salt. Heat the oil in a large skillet or dutch oven. Add the chicken and sauté over medium heat, turning occasionally, until skin is golden brown. Remove chicken and set aside. Add butter to pan and gently sauté the onion until soft, about 5 minutes. Add the garlic and cook over medium low heat for another minute. Do not let the garlic blacken. Stir in the nutmeg and cayenne pepper. Add the cooked chicken pieces and tomato sauce. Add water or chicken broth to the pan. Bring to a boil, cover, and lower heat to a simmer. Cook until chicken is tender and cooked through. Remove chicken to serving platter; keep warm. Meanwhile, stir peanut butter into sauce until it is smooth. Adjust seasonings, adding more salt, spice, or pepper to taste. Pour sauce over chicken. Serve with white rice.

FUFU

This Central African staple is usually made with cassava, or yucca, tubers; yams (not the sweet potatoes that Americans call yams), or yam flour; and sometimes plantains.

Here are two versions. The cassava flour version is more authentic, though in Africa, many cooks begin with the raw tubers themselves, which is more labor intensive. The second version is an adaptation for American cooks, using easily available materials, but takes a little longer to cook. The taste will not be quite the same.

3 cups (240 grams) cassava or tapioca flour (also known as tapioca starch in a more refined version and available from Bob's Red Mill and other brands, online, or in African or Caribbean markets. It may also be called "fufu powder.")

or

2 ½ cups (250 g) instant mashed potato flakes
2 ½ cups (300 g) baking mix, such as Bisquick

Bring six cups (1.4 liters) of water to a boil in a large pot. Add the cassava flour or the potato/baking mix combination, stir vigorously with a strong wooden spoon. If using cassava, stir for two minutes over low heat, or until very thick. If using the potato/baking mix, stir for 10—15 minutes. You may need two people—one to hold the pot and one to stir.

In either case, if the fufu seems thinner than mashed potatoes, add more of the dry ingredients. The fufu should be very thick but must be stirred constantly to avoid lumping and burning.

Shape the fufu into balls: Fill a bowl with water and empty, but do not dry. Set aside. When the dough is stiff, scoop 1 cup into the wet bowl and shake until it forms into a smooth ball. Serve on a large platter alongside a soup or stew. To eat, pull off a bite-sized piece, make an indentation in the center with a thumb or finger, then use it to scoop the stew. Serves 6—8.

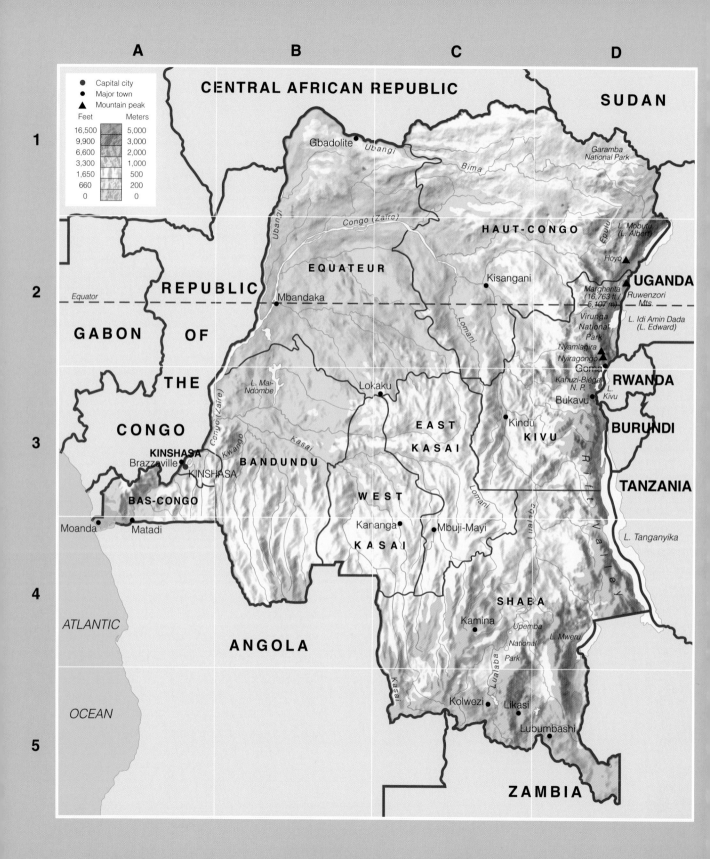

MAP OF DRC

Angola, A4—A5, B4—B5, C4—C5
Atlantic Ocean, A3—A5

Bandundu, B3
Bas-Congo, A3
Bima River, C1
Bukavu, D3
Burundi, D3

Central African Republic, A1, B1, C1
Congo (Zaire) River, A3, B2—B3, C2

East Kasai, C3
Epulu River, D1—D2

Gabon, A2—A3
Gambara National Park, D1
Gbadolite, B1
Goma, D2

Haut-Congo, C2, D2
Hoyo (Mountain), D2

Kahuzi-Biéga National Park, D3
Kamina, C4
Kananga, C4
Kasai River, B3—B4, C4—C5
Kindu, C3
Kinshaha (capital city), A3
Kinshaha (province), A2—B3
Kisangani, C2
Kivu, C3, D3
Kolwezi, C5
Kwango River, B3

Lake Kivu, D3
Lake Ldi Amin Dada (L. Edward), D2
Lake Mai-Ndombe, B3
Lake Mobutu (L. Albert), D2
Lake Mweru, D4
Lake Tanganyika, D4
Likasi, C5
Lokaku, C3
Lomani, C2—C3
Lualaba, C4—C5, D4—D5

Lubumbashi, D5

Margherita (Mountain), D2
Mbandaka, B2
Mbuji-Mayi, C4
Moanda, A4

Nyamlagira (Mountain), D2
Nyiragongo (Mountain), D2

Republic of the Congo, A2—A3, B1—B2
Rift Valley, D3—D4
Ruwenzori Mountains, D2
Rwanda, D2—D3

Shaba, C4, D4
Sudan, D1

Tanzania, D2—D4

Ubangi River, B1—B2, C1
Uganda, D1—D2
Upemba National Park, C4, D4

Virunga National Park, D2

West Kasai, B3—B4, C3—C4

Zambia, C5, D4—D5

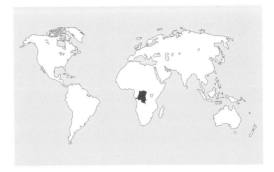

ECONOMIC DRC

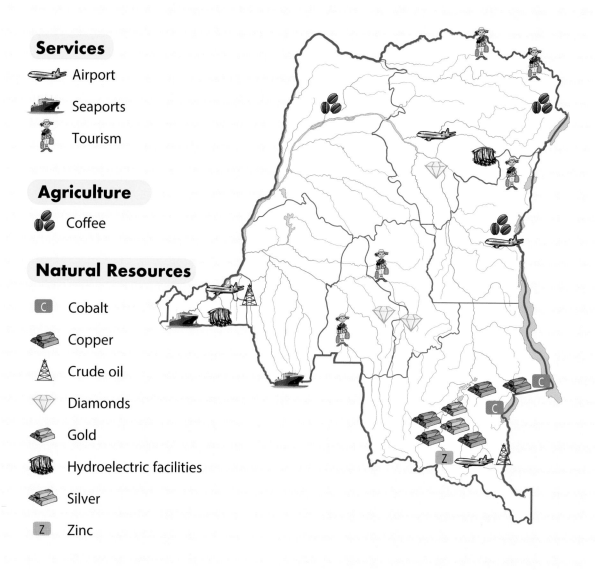

Services
- ✈ Airport
- 🚢 Seaports
- 🧳 Tourism

Agriculture
- ☕ Coffee

Natural Resources
- C Cobalt
- 🪙 Copper
- ⚒ Crude oil
- 💎 Diamonds
- 🪙 Gold
- ⛏ Hydroelectric facilities
- 🪙 Silver
- Z Zinc

ABOUT THE ECONOMY

GDP, OFFICIAL EXCHANGE RATE
$39.32 billion (2016)

GDP GROWTH RATE
2.4 percent (2016)

GDP COMPOSITION BY SECTOR
agriculture: 21.1 percent
industry: 32.7 percent
services: 46.3 percent (2016)

LAND USE
Agriculture 11 percent;
forest/woodland 67.9 percent;
other 20.7 percent (2011)

CURRENCY
Congolese franc (CDF); US$1 = 1596 CDF
(January 2018)

NATURAL RESOURCES
cobalt, copper, niobium, tantalum,
petroleum, industrial and gem diamonds,
gold, silver, zinc, manganese, tin, uranium,
coal, hydropower, timber

AGRICULTURAL PRODUCTS
coffee, sugar, palm oil, rubber, tea, cotton,
cocoa, quinine, cassava (manioc, tapioca),
bananas, plantains, peanuts, root crops,
corn, fruits; wood products

MAJOR EXPORTS
diamonds, copper, gold, cobalt, wood
products, crude oil, coffee

MAJOR IMPORTS
Foodstuffs, mining and other machinery,
transport equipment, fuels

MAIN TRADE PARTNERS
China, South Africa, Zambia, South Korea,
Saudi Arabia, Belgium

LABOR FORCE
30.31 million (2016)

UNEMPLOYMENT RATE
46.1 percent (2013)

INFLATION RATE
18.2 percent (2016)

POPULATION BELOW POVERTY LINE
63 percent (2012)

CULTURAL DRC

Luki Forest Reserve
This reserve has a humid tropical rain forest ecosystem. It is 492–1,640 feet (150–500 m) above sea level and has many habitats including primary forests, secondary forests, and savanna. The main economic activities here are agriculture and forestry.

Boyoma Falls
Formerly known as Stanley Falls, they consist of seven large, powerful waterfalls extending over 6 miles (9.7 km) along a curve of the Lualaba River. They currently hold the record of water flow, their average being 600,000 cubic feet (16,990 cubic m) a second.

Kinkole Fish Market
The fish market at Kinkole was constructed by Mobutu as part of his "authenticity" campaign to honor the country's fishermen. One can hire a pirogue for $10 an hour and be paddled down the Congo River.

Zongo Falls
The falls of Zongo are situated in the western province of Bas-Congo about 81 miles (130 km) from Kinshasa. They are surrounded by forest, and the rainfall from the volume of water crashing down produces a rainbow—an unforgettable sight.

Chutes de Lukia
A must for visitors in Kinshasa, the Chutes de Lukia have natural lakes to swim in and a bonobo orphanage to protect this rare species from the poachers. Visitors can cuddle the young bonobos.

Kinsato Botanical Gardens
The Kisanto Botanical Gardens in Matadi are a two-hour drive from Kinshasa. They feature a collection of 100-year-old trees from all over the world and rivers in which visitors can take a dip and rejuvenate themselves.

Kahuzi-Biéga National Park
Kahuzi-Biéga National Park is one of the last refuges of the rare mountain gorilla. The park was inscribed as a UNESCO World Heritage Site in 1980. The park is named after two extinct volcanoes, Mount Kahuzi and Mount Biéga.

Garamba National Park
Designated a UNESCO World Heritage Site in 1980, Garamba is home to the world's last known wild population of northern white rhinoceroses. The park is also well known for its African elephant domestication program, which started in the 1960s.

Rwenzori Mountains
The Rwenzori Mountains are a spectacular mountain range of Central Africa. The highest Rwenzoris are permanently snow-capped, the only such mountains, except for Mount Kilimanjaro and Mount Kenya, in Africa. The Rwenzori are known for their spectacular biodiversity.

Mount Nyiragongo
Mount Nyiragongo is a live volcano located in Virunga National Park, in the extreme east of the Democratic Republic of the Congo near the border of Rwanda. It erupted as recently as 2002 and has an impressive lake of red lava.

Lake Kivu
Lake Kivu is one of the great lakes of Africa. The lake bed sits upon Rift Valley, which is slowly being pulled apart and is surrounded by majestic mountains. The world's 10th-largest inland island, Idjwi, lies in Lake Kivu.

Upemba National Park
Upemba National Park is a large park in Katanga Province, located in a lush area dotted by lakes. It is home to some 1,800 species of animals, and there are also a handful of villages in the park.

ABOUT THE CULTURE

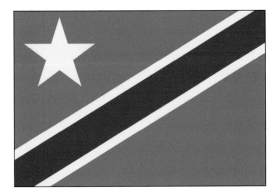

OFFICIAL NAME
République Démocratique du Congo
(Democratic Republic of the Congo)

FLAG DESCRIPTION
The DRC flag features a sky-blue
background, a yellow star in the upper left
corner, and a diagonal red stripe with a
yellow band down the middle.

TOTAL AREA
905,563 square miles (2,345,397 sq. km)

CAPITAL
Kinshasa

POPULATION
83,301,150 (2017)

ETHNIC GROUPS
The DRC has more than 200 African ethnic
groups, of which the majority are Bantu;
the four largest tribes—Mongo, Luba,
Kongo (all Bantu), and Mangbetu-Azande
(Hamitic)—make up about 45 percent of
the population.

RELIGION
Catholic 50 percent, Protestant 20
percent, Kimbanguist 10 percent, Muslim
10 percent, other syncretic sects and
traditional beliefs, 10 percent

BIRTH RATE
33.5 births per 1,000 Congolese (2017)

DEATH RATE
9.6 deaths per 1,000 Congolese (2017)

INFANT MORTALITY RATE
68.2 deaths per 1,000 live births (2017)

LIFE EXPECTANCY AT BIRTH
Total, 57.7 years
Male, 56.1 years
Female, 59.3 years (2017)

MAIN LANGUAGES
French (official), Lingala (a lingua franca),
Kingwana (a dialect of Kiswahili or
Swahili), Kikongo, Tshiluba

LITERACY
People aged 15 and older who can both
read and write French, Lingala, Kingwana,
or Tshiluba: Total population, 77 percent
Male, 88.5 percent
Female, 66.5 percent (2016)

TIMELINE

IN THE DRC	IN THE WORLD
1200s Rise of Kongo empire.	**1206** Genghis Khan unifies the Mongols and begins conquest of the world.
16th–17th centuries Europeans engage in slave trade out of Kongo.	**1558–1603** Reign of Elizabeth I of England
	1776 US Declaration of Independence
	1861–1865 US Civil War
1874–1877 Henry Stanley explores Central Africa.	
1870s King Léopold II of Belgium begins colonization of Congo.	
1884–1885 European powers recognize Léopold's claim to the Congo Basin.	
1885 Léopold II announces the establishment of the Congo Free State, headed by him.	
1891–1892 Belgians conquer Katanga.	
1908 Congo Free State placed under Belgian rule.	**1914–1919** World War I
	1939–1945 World War II
	1949 The North Atlantic Treaty Organization (NATO) is formed.
1960 Congo becomes independent. Patrice Lamumba is named prime minister. Congolese army mutinies.	
1961 Patrice Lamumba is assassinated.	
1965 President and prime minister ousted in a coup led by Joseph Mobutu.	**1969** Neil Armstrong becomes the first human to walk on the moon.
1971 Mobutu renames the country Zaire and himself Mobutu Sese Seko.	**1986** Nuclear power disaster at Chernobyl in Ukraine
	1991 Breakup of the Soviet Union

IN DRC		IN THE WORLD
1997		
Rebels oust Mobutu. Laurent Kabila becomes president. Zaire renamed the DRC.		
1997–2003		
Second Congo War		
2001		**2001**
President Laurent Kabila is assassinated. Joseph Kabila succeeds his father.		Terrorists attack the US on 9/11.
2006		**2003**
New constitution and new flag are adopted. The first free elections in four decades are held; Joseph Kabila wins the presidency.		War in Iraq begins.
2008		**2008**
Conflicts continue in eastern provinces, creating a refugee crisis.		US elects first African American president, Barack Obama.
2011		
Joseph Kabila wins another term in disputed election.		
2012		
M23 rebel group attacks eastern provinces, and captures Goma.		
2013		
Eleven African countries pledge to help end the conflict in the DRC. M23 signs a peace deal with government.		
2014		
Congolese and Rwandan troops clash on the border of their two countries.		**2015–2016**
2016		ISIS launches terror attacks in Belgium and France.
Presidential election is delayed.		
2017		**2017**
Electoral commission schedules elections for December 2018.		Donald Trump becomes US president. Hurricanes devastate Houston, Caribbean islands, and Puerto Rico.
2018		**2018**
UN declares "dramatic deterioration" of the humanitarian situation in DRC and launches largest-ever funding appeal for assistance.		Winter Olympics in South Korea

GLOSSARY

amicales (AM-ee-KAHL)
Fraternal associations for workers in the mid-1950s.

bushmeat
the meat of African wild animals; often used to describe the meat of endangered mammals illegally hunted for food

cassava
Root used as a staple food; also called manioc.

gumbo
Young okra pods used as a staple vegetable; turns slimy when cooked.

Jamaa
A religious movement.

Jambo (YAM-boh)
"Hello" in Kiswahili.

Jambosana (YAM-boh SAH-nah)
"Hello very much" in Kiswahili.

kalimba (ka-LIM-bah)
Thumb piano with hand-plucked metal strips set against a wooden soundboard.

Kiswahili
Widely used language in the eastern border region and in Lubumbashi in the southeast.

kleptocracy
Government system that includes bribery, corruption, and the systemic embezzlement of public funds.

kwasakwasa (KWA-sa KWA-sa)
A kind of music enjoyed by the Kinshasans.

kwashiorkor
A protein-deficiency disease that stunts growth and causes the muscles to waste away.

li (lee)
Evil spirit believed to reside in the stomach of certain people.

Lingala
A Congolese language.

lingua franca
Any language that is widely used as a means of communication among speakers of other languages.

mankala (man-KAH-la)
National board game of the DRC.

mbote (m-BOH-tay)
"Hello" in Lingala.

nganda (un-GAN-dah)
Congolese bar offering dancing and drinking.

pillage (pee-YAHJ)
French word referring to the looting of shops and houses, especially during a time of chaos and disorder.

pirogue
A canoe made from a hollow tree.

savanna
A grassland region.

Shauriya Mungu (SHOW-reeyoh MUN-goo)
"It is God's will."

FOR FURTHER INFORMATION

BOOKS

Butcher, Tim. *Blood River: The Terrifying Journey Through The World's Most Dangerous Country.* New York: Grove Press, 2009.

Greenbaum, Eli. *Emerald Labyrinth: A Scientist's Adventures in the Jungles of the Congo.* Lebanon, NH: ForeEdge, 2017.

Hochschild, Adam. *King Leopold's Ghost: A Story of Greed, Terror, and Heroism in Colonial Africa.* New York: Houghton Mifflin, 1999.

Sterns, Jason. *Dancing in the Glory of Monsters: The Collapse of the Congo and the Great War of Africa.* New York: PublicAffairs, 2011.

Uwiringiyimana, Sandra. *How Dare the Sun Rise: Memoirs of a War Child.* New York: Katherine Tegen Books, HarperCollins, 2017.

ONLINE

BBC. DR Congo country profile. http://www.bbc.com/news/world-africa-13283212

____ Democratic Republic of the Congo profile, Timeline. http://www.bbc.com/news/world-africa-13286306

CIA World Factbook, Democratic Republic of the Congo. https://www.cia.gov/library/publications/the-world-factbook/geos/cg.html

Encyclopaedia Britannica. Democratic Republic of the Congo. https://www.britannica.com/place/Democratic-Republic-of-the-Congo

Mongabay, Congo archives. https://news.mongabay.com/?s=Congo

New York Times, The. Congo archives. https://www.nytimes.com/topic/destination/congo

FILMS

Nightline. *Heart of Darkness: The Democratic Republic of Congo*. ABC News, 2006.

Lumo. Goma Film Project, 2006.

MUSIC

Kolosoy, Wendo. *The Very Best of Congolese Rumba*.Marabi France, 2008.

Ngo, Samba: *Ndoto*. Samba Ngo Production, 2003.

Rumbanella Band: *El Congo: Congolese Rumba*. Melodie, 2003.

BIBLIOGRAPHY

Al Jazeera. "Democratic Republic of Congo News." http://www.aljazeera.com/topics/country/posting_under_country.html.

BBC Magazine. "Is the Holy Spirit Living in Africa?" July 11, 2015. http://www.bbc.com/news/magazine-33476886.

CIA World Factbook. "Democratic Republic of the Congo." https://www.cia.gov/library/publications/the-world-factbook/geos/cg.html.

Cordell, Dennis D., Ntsomo Payanzo, Bernd Michael Wiese, and René Lemarchand. Democratic Republic of the Congo. *Encyclopaedia Britannica*. https://www.britannica.com/place/Democratic-Republic-of-the-Congo.

Draper, Robert. "The Main Road Through the Heart of Africa Is the Congo River—For Those Who Dare to Take It." *National Geographic*, October 2015. http://ngm.nationalgeographic.com/2015/10/congo-river/draper-text.

Evans, Kate. "Bushmeat Stories: Voices from the Congo Basin." *Our World*, November 23, 2012. https://ourworld.unu.edu/en/bushmeat-stories-voices-from-the-congo-basin.

Gottipati, Sruthi. "In Congo, Artists Rely on the Patronage of the Wealthy." *Al Jazeera*, June 17, 2017. http://www.aljazeera.com/indepth/features/2017/05/congo-artists-rely-patronage-wealthy-170529092655899.html.

Jasanoff, Maya. "With Conrad on the Congo River." *The New York Times*, August 18, 2017. https://www.nytimes.com/2017/08/18/opinion/joseph-conrad-congo-river.html.

Murori, Kajuju. "Seven Top Reasons Why Africa Is Still Poor, 2017." *The African Exponent*, February 17, 2016. https://www.africanexponent.com/post/billions-lost-in-profits-by-foreign-companies-tax-evasion-1953

OSAC. "Democratic Republic of the Congo 2017 Crime and Safety Report." https://www.osac.gov/pages/ContentReportDetails.aspx?cid=21576.

Trading Economics. "Congo Unemployment Rate." https://tradingeconomics.com/congo/unemployment-rate.

UNAIDS. "Democratic Republic of the Congo Factsheets 2016." http://www.unaids.org/en/regionscountries/countries/democraticrepublicofthecongo.

UNICEF. "Democratic Republic of the Congo: Statistics." https://www.unicef.org/infobycountry/drcongo_statistics.html.

World Food Programme. "Democratic Republic of the Congo." http://www1.wfp.org/countries/democratic-republic-congo.

Zongwe, Dunia P., François Butedi and Phebe Mavungu Clément. "UPDATE: The Legal System of the Democratic Republic of the Congo (DRC): Overview and Research." Hauser Global Law School Program. January/February 2015. http://www.nyulawglobal.org/globalex/Democratic_Republic_Congo1.html.

INDEX

Africa, 5, 9—11, 14, 18, 22—23, 25, 28—29, 33, 37, 44, 49—50, 54—55, 57, 59—60, 65, 69, 71, 74—75, 84, 87—88, 90, 92—93, 95, 97—99, 101, 103—104, 106—107, 109, 111, 113, 122, 125, 129, 131
Africanization, 29, 42, 52, 92, 97, 119
agriculture, 19, 50—51, 55, 57, 59, 90, 122
AIDS, 81, 84—85, 107, 125
animals, 5, 8, 18, 25, 57—64, 73, 78—79, 82, 106, 113, 121—122, 125, 127

Belgian Congo, 27, 50—51, 89, 92, 99
Belgians, 13, 39—40, 79
Belgium, 9, 14, 25—28, 34, 39—40, 89, 98
bonobos, 19, 21, 59, 64, 125
Brazzaville, 10—11, 26, 55
bushmeat, 58—60, 67, 125—126, 129

cassava, 51, 70—71, 79—80, 124, 126—129, 131
Catholic, 31, 35, 41, 81, 87—89, 91—93, 118—119
Cheybeya, Floribert, 36
children, 6, 26, 70—71, 73, 77, 81—85, 89—90, 111—114, 117—118, 122—123, 127
chimpanzees, 19, 58—59, 67, 84, 125, 129
Christianity, 24, 70, 87—89, 106
colonial, 5, 12, 23, 27, 31, 39—40, 42, 73, 95, 97—98, 117
Congo Free State, 26, 39, 98
Congo River, 9—12, 16, 19, 21, 24—26, 33, 54—55, 64, 70, 78—79, 85, 87, 91, 96, 106, 114, 128
constitution, 35, 40, 42—47, 118
corruption, 6, 15, 23, 34—35, 42, 45, 49, 54, 64, 77
crime, 13, 77

dance, 91, 101—104, 115—116
diamonds, 15, 23, 28, 33, 36, 49, 51—52, 55
disease, 6, 15, 36, 60, 66, 83—84, 124—125

electricity, 11—12, 16, 49, 52—55, 82, 103—104, 128
elephants, 5, 18, 58, 61, 63—64, 125
Europe, 23, 25, 87, 104, 121
European, 5, 23—25, 28—29, 32, 36, 53, 71, 89, 95—96, 98, 103

famine, 122
fetishes, 90, 105—106
floods, 11
folktale, 114
food, 19, 50—51, 59—60, 73—74, 77, 80, 82—83, 85, 111, 114, 120—127
food insecurity, 85, 123—124
forests, 5, 10, 15—19, 21, 49, 57—62, 64—65, 67, 70—71, 73, 75, 78, 80, 83, 91, 105—106, 125
French, 26, 30, 34, 71, 82, 84, 88, 95, 97—99, 104, 128
fufu (recipe), 131

Gbadolite, 16, 21, 30—31
GDP, 49—50
gold, 13, 17, 23, 30, 36, 48, 51, 99, 118
gorillas, 5, 17, 19, 58—62, 65, 67, 125
Grand Inga Dam, 54—55
Great Lakes, 17, 20, 32—33

health, 49, 65, 82—83, 85, 92, 99, 112, 121—122
humanitarian, 6—7, 36, 85, 112, 122—123
human rights, 6, 30, 36, 44, 46
hunger, 6, 85, 122—123, 126
hydroelectric, 11, 49, 52—55

independence, 5, 25, 27—28, 34, 40—41, 44, 50, 52, 92, 99, 117

Ituri Forest, 15, 59, 61—62, 73, 75, 91

Kabila, Joseph, 7, 35—36, 42, 44, 47, 87, 92
Kabila, Laurent, 16, 33—35, 41—42, 70, 99, 117
Kasavubu, Joseph, 27—29, 31, 41
Katanga, 13, 24, 27—29, 34, 40—41, 51, 64, 70, 72, 89, 97, 108, 123
Kikongo, 71, 89, 96—97
Kimbangu, Simon, 89—90, 93
Kimbanguist church, 89—90
Kinshasa, 10—14, 16, 25—26, 29—31, 33, 36, 38, 43, 53, 55, 66, 71—72, 78—80, 82, 88, 95—98, 100—101, 106—108, 112—113, 115, 128—129
Kisangani, 10, 12, 14, 16—17, 29, 33, 41, 53, 78, 80, 82, 96—97, 128
Kongo, 5, 24—25, 71, 87, 89, 96, 106—107

Lake Tanganyika, 14, 17—18
Léopold II, King, 14, 25—26, 39
Léopoldville, 12, 27, 31, 97
Lingala, 71, 82, 84, 96, 98—99, 104
Livingstone, David, 14, 25, 54
logging, 15, 19, 58—59, 61, 64, 67, 125
Lubumbashi, 13, 33, 51, 53, 70, 80, 82, 89, 96—97, 107, 113
Lumumba, Patrice, 27—29, 31, 34, 40—41, 117

M23 (rebel group), 17
mabanga, 102, 109
malnutrition, 6, 36, 122—123, 127
mankala, 110—113, 115
mazuku (poison gases), 20
Mbuji-Mayi, 13, 33, 52, 80
minerals, 5, 13, 15, 23, 26, 51—52, 58, 124
mining, 13, 15, 17, 28—29, 30, 33, 37, 51—52, 55, 58—59, 70, 113, 125
missionaries, 24, 26, 29, 31, 70, 81, 87, 91—92, 96

INDEX

Mobutu Sese Seko, 16, 28—31, 33—34, 39, 41—42, 44, 52, 71, 92—93, 97, 99, 113, 117—119
mountains, 5, 9, 10—11, 17—18, 21, 60, 62, 65, 76
Mukwege, Dennis, 7
music, 5, 80, 101—104, 109
Mutombo, Dikembe, 112, 115

national parks, 17—18, 56—57, 60—65, 125
natural resources, 36, 49, 64

okapi, 16, 57—59, 61—62

Papa Wemba, 104, 109
poaching, 19, 37, 57, 59—65, 125
Poulet a la moambe (chicken groundnut or peanut stew) (recipe), 130
poverty, 6, 23, 49, 77, 80, 102, 126
pygmies, 62, 69, 73, 75, 80, 91

rebels, 17, 29, 32—33
refugees, 17, 32, 57, 60—61, 69, 74—75
rhinos, 63, 67
rivers, 5, 9—13, 15—16, 19, 21—22, 24—26, 31, 33, 52—55, 58, 64—66, 70—73, 77—80, 85, 87, 90—91, 96—98, 106, 108, 114, 128
roads, 6, 17—18, 25—26, 40, 51—52, 55, 64, 78, 85, 125
rumba, 103—104, 109
Rwanda/Rwandans, 9, 17—18, 20, 32—34, 36, 51, 57, 62, 65, 69, 74
Rwenzori Mountains, 18, 21

schools, 24, 31, 77, 81—82, 88, 91, 95, 119
Second Congo War, 5, 17, 33, 36, 46
slavery, 25, 39, 69, 73
soccer, 111, 113
Soviet Union, 28, 41
Stanley, Henry Morton, 14—18, 25, 107
starvation, 6, 25, 77, 101, 124

Swahili, 20, 34, 70, 95—97, 99, 111

tourism, 17, 20, 62, 65, 108
Tshisekedi, Etienne, 35, 41
Tshombe, Moïse, 29, 40—41

UNICEF, 70, 82, 85, 102, 121, 123
United Nations, 6—7, 28—29, 37, 41, 44, 47
United States, 9, 28—29, 36, 41, 50, 69, 84, 112, 121

violence, 6—7, 23, 27, 32, 36—37, 40, 51, 57, 63—64, 85, 88, 90, 107, 125
Virunga National Park, 17—18, 56—57, 60—62, 65, 67

wars, 5—7, 14, 17, 23, 28, 32—34, 36—37, 41, 46, 49, 52, 57, 60, 63, 65—66, 81—82, 85, 123—124
wildlife, 5, 16, 18, 21, 57, 59, 61—63, 79, 125
women, 7, 15, 44, 71, 73, 75, 80, 82—83, 85, 89, 99, 114, 124

Zaire, 9—11, 29—30, 32—34, 41, 53, 60, 92, 97—99, 113, 117